Ships from Scotland to America, 1628–1828

Volume IV

Ships
from SCOTLAND
to AMERICA

1628 – 1828

Volume IV

By David Dobson

CLEARFIELD

Printed for Clearfield Company by
Genealogical Publishing Company
Baltimore, Maryland
2010

ISBN 978-0-8063-5511-5

Made in the United States of America

INTRODUCTION

One of the more difficult tasks encountered by genealogists in North America is establishing how and when their immigrant ancestor arrived from Scotland. This is particularly true for the seventeenth and eighteenth centuries, periods for which records are far from comprehensive. If the vessel that the immigrant sailed on can be identified, then the ports of arrival and departure may also follow, and this in turn may indicate the locality from which the immigrant originated, thus narrowing the search. Information pertaining to the ship that brought one's immigrant ancestor is an essential feature of a comprehensive family history. What kind of ship was it? What was its tonnage? Where was it registered? Who was the skipper? All these questions are of interest to the family historian and are partially answered in this book.

This book is designed as an aid to the family historian by identifying ships from Scotland to what is now the United States and Canada for the period 1628 to 1828. Evidence of direct shipping between Scotland and the Americas can be established as early as 1600 when the *Grace of God* returned to Dundee from Newfoundland. Links with the West Indies date from 1611 and the voyage of the *Janet of Leith,* and with the Chesapeake with the *Golden Lion of Dundee,* which sailed via London in 1626. All these , however, are believed to have been trading voyages. Emigration to America from Scotland began with the attempt by Sir William Alexander to settle Nova Scotia in the 1620s. It is believed that although there were a number of vessels which could be described as "emigrant ships", the majority of emigrants during our period went on cargo ships. There seems to have been a continuous trickle of emigrants across the Atlantic from the mid–seventeenth century onwards, to staff the tobacco warehouses in Virginia, for example, or as felons banished to the Plantations. Economic forces generally determined emigrant routes from Scotland: ships sailed to Georgia and the Carolinas for cotton and rice, to the Chesapeake for tobacco, to the Canadian Maritimes for timber, and carried with them innumerable emigrants, many as indentured servants. The significant rise in emigration from Great Britain, especially from the Scottish Highlands, that occurred in the decade before the American Revolution resulted in the British government maintaining a Register of Emigrants. This, albeit incomplete, covers the period 1773 to 1774 and identifies who emigrated, how they emigrated, why they emigrated, when they emigrated, plus their ports of departure and destinations. The only similar large scale emigration occurred in the years after the end of the Napoleonic Wars when thousands if Scots sailed from the Clyde bound for Canada. Apart from these two periods the picture is far from complete. Passenger arrival records in the United States and Canada are sometimes vague and identify the port of origin as "Scotland" or "North Britain". This is particularly true in the case of emigrant ships that sailed from remote bays or inlets in the Highlands and Islands where the catchment area for emigrants was highly localized. By the early nineteenth century Greenock had become the major port for emigrants from all over Scotland, but ships did sail from other ports, and their passengers are highly likely to have come from their immediate neighbourhoods.

Volume IV of *Ships from Scotland to America, 1628-1828* unlike volumes I and II, but like volume III, contains a number of vessels bound from Scotland to the West Indies. It also contains mention of a number of early ships that arrived in Scotland from the colonies, some presumably on the return voyage, while some were colonial vessels which would then return across the Atlantic.

David Dobson

Dundee, Scotland

REFERENCES

Archives

ACA	=	Aberdeen City Archives
DA	=	Dundee Archives
DGA	=	Dumfries & Galloway Archives
NA	=	National Archives, London
NARA	=	National Archives, Records Administration
NAS	=	National Archives of Scotland
NSARM	=	Nova Scotia Archives & Record Management
PANB	=	Public Archives of New Brunswick

Publications

ActsPCCol		Acts of the Privy Council Colonial, series [London, 1912]
BoNL	=	Boston Newsletter, series
BSL	=	Boston Shipping Lists, series
CC	=	Canadian Courant, series
CCMA	=	Canadian Courant & Montreal Advertiser
CM	=	Caledonian Mercury, series
CW	=	Colonial Williamsburg
DBR	=	Dumfries Burgh Records
GA	=	Greenock Advertiser, series
GCt	=	Glasgow Courant, series
GC	=	Glasgow Courier, series
GHG	=	History of Glasgow, J. Gibson [Glasgow, 1777]
L	=	Lloyd's Register, series
MG	=	Montreal Gazette, series
MH	=	Montreal Herald, series
QGaz	=	Quebec Gazette, series
QM	=	Quebec Mercury, series
RPCS	=	Register of the Privy Council of Scotland, series
SC	=	Scots Courant, series
VG	=	Virginia Gazette, series
VSS	=	Virginia Slave Statistics, [Richmond, 1984]

SHIPS FROM SCOTLAND TO AMERICA 1628-1828

Volume IV

ABERDEENSHIRE, Captain Oswald, from Aberdeen to Halifax, Nova Scotia, in July 1826; from Aberdeen to Pictou, Nova Scotia, in August 1827. [NAS.E504.1.32]

ACHILLES, master William Wood, from Greenock *with passengers* bound for Jamaica in January 1802, sailed 16 March 1802. [GA#2/20]

ACTIVE, Captain Campbell, from the Clyde to Boston 23 September 1802. [GA#1/76]

ACTIVE, master A.Walker, arrived in Quebec during September 1827 *with 40 passengers* from Tobermory, Mull. [QM:21.9.1827]

ADAH, from Dundee to Jamaica in October 1828 and in October 1829. [NAS.E504.11.26]

ADAM AND BETTY OF INVERKEITHING, 60 tons, master David Inglis, from Leith to Grenada in December 1764. [NAS.E504.22.11]

ADVENTURE OF GLASGOW, a brigantine, master Thomas Fisher, from Port Glasgow to Madeira in August 1691. [NAS.E72.19.22]

ADVENTURE, a snow, master ....Ferguson, arrived in the James River, Virginia, in July 1746 from Dumfries. [VG:11.7.1746]

ADVENTURE OF AYR, master John McIlraith, from Ayr to Barbados in December 1746. [NAS.E504.4.1]

ADVENTURE OF GLASGOW, from Port Glasgow via Cork to Jamaica in January 1749. [NAS,E504.28.4]

ADVENTURE OF LEITH, 100 tons, master James Hamilton, from Leith to Jamaica in January 1754. [NAS.E504.22.5]

ADVENTURE OF LONDON, master Andrew Smith, from Kirkcaldy to Antigua in June 1772, [NAS.E504.20.8]

ADVENTURE, master Thomas Symmers, from Aberdeen *with passengers* to Barbados, Tobago, and Grenada, on 12 April 1774. [AJ#1360/1373]

AGAMEMNON, Captain Rogers, arrived in Quebec on 17 August 1818, *with 192 passengers* from Leith. [QM: 15.8.1818][MG]

AGINCOURT, Captain Matheson, arrived in Quebec on 2 August 1818 *with 298 passengers* from Leith. [MG]

AGNES OF GLASGOW, a galley, master Patrick Galbreath, from Port Glasgow to Antigua in February 1709; master Andrew Turbet, from Port Glasgow to Barbados in October 1716. [NAS.E508.2.6/10.6]

AGNES, master Robert Schaw, from Ayr to Barbados in October 1755. [NAS.E504.4.2]

AGNES, from Leith on 6 April 1822, arrived in Quebec on 11 June 1822; Captain Mackay, arrived in Quebec on 25 May 1823 from Leith. [MG:15.6.1822][CC:31.5.1823]

AGNES AND JEAN OF AYR, arrived in Greenock on 26 May 1741 from Virginia. [CM#3305]

AGNES AND JOHN OF AYR, master Ged Gordon, from Ayr, via Cork, Madeira and Barbados to Virginia in 1728. [NA.CO.33.16]

AIMWELL, Captain Hanna, from Greenock to Tobago in January 1802, sailed 7 February 1802. [GA#2/8]

AJAX, master Alexander MacLaurin, from Leith via Madeira to Black River and Savanna la Mar, Jamaica, 1802. *"tradesmen, husbandmen, etc, will meet with good encouragement to go by the above ship."* [CM:9.10.1802]

ALBANY OF GLASGOW, from Virginia via Barbados and Jamaica to Inverness, in 1722. [NAS.AC8.285]

ALBANY OF GLASGOW, master William Gemmell, from the Clyde to Virginia in 1735; arrived in the James River, Virginia, on 26 June 1738 from Greenock; master John Lyon, arrived in the Upper District of the James River, Virginia, on 4 May 1739 from Glasgow. [GHG#210][VG:30.6.1738][VaGaz#100/158]

ALBANY, master Richard Tucker, arrived in the James River, Virginia, on 25 August 1768 from Glasgow. [VG:1.9.1768]

ALBION, master G. Service, arrived in Quebec during September 1802 from Fort William *with passengers.* [QGaz: 11.9.1802]

ALBION, 152 tons, master Robert Kidd, arrived in Prince Edward Island on 14 June 1809 *with 39 passengers* from Dundee. [PAPEI/RG9]

ALBION, 250 ton brig, master William Jack, from Burghead to Kingston, Jamaica, *with passengers* in October 1824. [IC#355]

ALBION, from Aberdeen to Miramichi, New Brunswick, in July 1827. [NAS.E504.1.32]

ALDIE, master Peter Brown, from Leith to Grenada in December 1777. [AJ#1558]

ALERT, Captain Muir, from Campbeltown to New Richmond, Quebec, on 5 August 1823. [NAS.E504.8.10]

ALEXANDER, master William Ramsay, from Scotland to Nova Scotia in September 1628, returned to Loch Ryan. [NAS.AC7.2.117]

ALEXANDER OF INVERKEITHING, master Thomas Thomson, from Leith to Carolina and return in 1684. [NAS.AC7.8]

ALEXANDER OF LEITH, master Laurence Brown, from Leith to Grenada in December 1769, in April 1771, also in March 1772. [NAS.E504.22.7/15/16/17]

ALEXANDER, Captain Durham, from the Clyde to Newfoundland in April 1802. [GA#1/28]

ALEXANDER, arrived in Quebec on 22 July 1817 *with 44 passengers* from Leith. [MG]

ALEXANDER, Captain Young, arrived in Quebec on 5 June 1820 *with 96 passengers* from Greenock, [QM]; Captain Ferguson, arrived in Quebec on 5 September 1820 *with 112 passengers* from Greenock. [QM: 5.9.1820]

ALEXANDER, a 250 ton brig, from Kirkcaldy to Norfolk and Richmond, Virginia in April 1823. [DPCA#1078]

ALEXANDER, Captain Cummings, arrived in Quebec on 30 May 1820 *with 2 passengers* from Aberdeen on 3 April 1820, [QM]; Captain Carnegie, from Aberdeen to Quebec in April 1826, [NAS.E504.1.32]

ALEXIS, a brig, Captain Livingston, from Greenock to Wilmington, North Carolina, in July 1802. [GA#1/46]

ALLETTA OF RHODE ISLAND, master William Campbell, from Montrose, Angus, to Rhode Island on 5 December 1750. [NAS.E504.24.2]

ALLIANCE OF PITTENWEEM, 100 tons, master George Fortune, from Leith to Maryland in February 1753. [NAS.E504.22.5]

AMELIA OF NEW YORK, from Inverkeithing to New York in November 1810. [NAS.E504.16.1]

AMERICA OF GLASGOW, master James Scott, from the Clyde to Virginia in 1735, arrived in Port Glasgow on 14 November 1735 from Virginia. [GHG#210][NAS.E512/1455]; master

James Scott, from the Clyde to Virginia in 1737, [NAS.AC8.541]; master Robert Ritchie, arrived in Greenock from Virginia on 7 October 1739. [CM#3205]; arrived in Islay bound for Greenock from Virginia in September 1740; master Robert Ritchie, from Greenock to Virginia on 28 March 1741. [CM#5316/3279][EEC#5399]

AMERICAN MERCHANT OF PORT GLASGOW, 160 tons, arrived in the Clyde from Virginia in 1711. [SC: 21.4.1711]

AMERICAN PLANTER OF LEITH, master Robert Alexander, later John Laverock, from Leith to Charleston also to the Bay of Honduras, and return, 1773. [NAS.AC9.2779; E504.22.18]

AMITY OF BOSTON, master Lott Gordon, arrived in Port Glasgow on 31 August 1691 from New England. [NAS.E72.15.21]

AMITY OF GLASGOW, 130 tons, master George Blair, arrived in the York River, Virginia, on 16 February 1734 from Jamaica; from the Clyde to Jamaica in 1735. [GHG#210]; from Port Glasgow to Jamaica in February 1739. [CM#2932]; master James Weir, arrived in Greenock on 27 December 1740 from Virginia; arrived in Greenock on 20 February 1742 from Jamaica; from Greenock to Jamaica on 17 April 1742; from Port Glasgow and Greenock to Jamaica on 7 January 1743; master James Aitken, from Port Glasgow to Jamaica in November 1748. [NA.CO5/1320.R3][CM#3240/3350/3372] [NAS.E504.28.1/4; E504.15.1]

AMITY, Captain Ray, from Glasgow to Montreal in July 1829, [NAS.E504.13.57]; arrived in Quebec during August 1829 *with 17 passengers* from Glasgow. [QM: 29.8.1829]

AMSTERDAM PACKET, an American ship, from Greenock bound for New York in March 1802. [GA#16]

ANACREAN, Captain Wilson, arrived in Quebec on 21 October 1817 *with 93 passengers* from Tobermory. [MG: 29.10.1817]

ANDREW MCKEAN, Captain Irvine, from Inverkeithing to Quebec in July 1825. [NAS.E504.16.1]

ANDROMANCHE, an American ship, Captain Piercy, from Greenock to New York in July 1802. [GA#1/40/53]

ANDROMEDA, Captain Middleton, from Glasgow on 28 June 1825 bound for Quebec, arrived there on 18 August 1825. [CCMA: 24.8.1825]

ANN OF GLASGOW, a 85 ton galley, from Port Glasgow via Dublin to Barbados in November 1711; master James Barclay, from Port Glasgow to Barbados in November 1712 and in October 1713, [SC:24.11.1711][NA.HCA.26/15] [NAS.E508.7.6; E508.7.6]

ANN OF INVERNESS, a galley, master James Dauling, from Inverness to Barbados in September 1715, [NAS.E508.7.6] [NAS.AC7.8.196]

ANN OF EDINBURGH, master Robert Bryson, from Leith to Boston, New England, in 1736. [NAS.AC13.1.303; AC10.246; AC7.43.493; AC9.1417]

ANN OF GLASGOW, master Robert Denham, from Greenock to Virginia on 12 May 1741; arrived in Greenock on 13 February 1742 from Virginia; master William Smith, from Greenock to Virginia on 29 May 1742; master John Smith, arrived in Port Glasgow on 7 March 1743 from Virginia; master John Smith, from Greenock to Jamaica in June 1745; from Port Glasgow to Jamaica in September 1746. [CM#3299/3346/3391][NAS.E504.28.1/2; E504.15.2]

ANN OF ABERDEEN, master John Thomson, from Aberdeen to Virginia in March 1750. [NAS.E504.1.3]

ANN, master John Francis, from Greenock to Barbados in January 1763; master William Robison, from Greenock to Barbados in May 1766. [NAS.E504.15.11/13]

ANN, master James Leggat, from Port Glasgow to Halifax, Nova Scotia, in July 1777, [NAS.E504.28.27]

ANN, Captain Cochrane, from Greenock to Virginia on 19 February 1802. [GA#14]

ANN, from Cromarty *with passengers* to Pictou, Nova Scotia, in June 1818. [IC.29]

ANN, a brig, master William Duthie, from Peterhead on 14 April 1819, arrived in Quebec on 30 May 1819. [MG:9.6.1819]

ANN, master J. Redpath, from Greenock on 4 April 1822, arrived in Quebec on 17 May 1822; Captain Henry, from Glasgow on 31 July 1822 *with 26 passengers* bound for Quebec, arrived there on 12 October 1822; Captain MacLean, arrived in Quebec on 22 May 1823 *with 38 passengers* from Glasgow on 1 April 1823. [QM:30.5.1822; 23.5.1823][MG:19.10.1822] [CC:28.5.1823]

ANN, Captain Wilson, from Leith on 1 April 1825 bound for Quebec, arrived there on 25 May 1825. [CCMA:1.6.1825]

ANN OF CAMPBELTOWN, master Daniel McMurchy, from Campbeltown, Argyll, to New Richmond, Quebec, in April 1826. [NAS.E504.8.10]

ANN, from Port Glasgow to St John, New Brunswick, in August 1829. [NAS.E504.28.149]

ANN AND MARY, Captain Brown, from Greenock to Montreal on 13 April 1802. [GA#1/29]

ANN AND PEGGY OF EYEMOUTH, master Peter Dalgleish, from Kirkcaldy, Fife, to Grenada in March 1772. [NAS.E504.20.8]

ANNA OF GLASGOW, master James Barclay, arrived in Glasgow from Barbados in 1715. [NAS.AC8.196]

ANNABELLA, a snow, master Robert Hamilton, arrived at Hampton, Virginia, on 31 August 1745 from Glasgow.[VaGaz#480]

ANTELOPE OF ABERDEEN, from Aberdeen to Virginia in 1711. [SC:26.5.1711]

ANTELOPE, master Cabel Chapin, from the Clyde to the Chesapeake, Pennsylvania, and the West Indies, in 1693. [GA:Shawfield Mss.1/42-44][NAS.CS29/1752]

ARBROATH OF ARBROATH, master Patrick Gellatly, from Montrose, Angus, to Boston, New England, 14 June 1751. [NAS.E504.24.2]

ARCHIBALD, master Patrick Gordon, from Greenock to Grenada in January 1767. [NAS.E504.15.14]

ARDGOUR OF FORT WILLIAM, a 160 ton snow, Captain Leslie, from Fort William, Inverness-shire, *with 108 passengers* bound for Quebec, arrived there on 6 September 1817. [NAS.E504.12.6][QM:9.9.1817][MG]

ARGUS, a brig, from Dumfries to Prince Edward Island on May 1820; Captain Wilkinson, arrived in Quebec on 14 August 1820 *with 88 passengers* from Dumfries. [DWJ.30.5.1820][QM: 14.8.1820]

ARGYLE OF GLASGOW, master William Watson, from the Clyde to Antigua in 1735. [GHG#210]; master John MacCun, from Greenock to Virginia on 4 October 1740. [CM#3204]; master William Montgomery, from Port Glasgow to Antigua in December 1743; from Port Glasgow to Antigua and Jamaica in March 1745; from Port Glasgow to Antigua in 1747; from Port Glasgow to Antigua in October 1748. [NAS.E504.28.1/2/3/4]

ARGYLE OF LEITH, 150 tons, master Dougal Matheson, from Kirkcaldy, Fife, to Tobago in February 1773; from Leith to Tobago in January 1774. [NAS.E504.20.8; E504.22.18]

ARGYLE, a brigantine, master Charles Cunningham, from Greenock to Jamaica in February 1765; arrived in Savannah, Georgia, on 25 January 1766 from Jamaica. [NAS.E504.15.12][NA.CO5/709]

ARGYLL OF CAMPBELTOWN, master Samuel Huie, from Campbeltown, Argyll, to Philadelphia on 9 July 1753. [NAS.E504.8.2]

ARGYLL, master William Walkinshaw, from Greenock to Jamaica in January 1767, [NAS.E504.15.14]

ARIADNE, Captain Johnston, from the Clyde to Barbados 24 September 1802. [GA#1/76]

ARIEL, 234 ton brig, master Duncan Ritchie, from Greenock to New York in November 1822, [EEC#17,369]

ATLANTIC, 213 tons, master Neil McIntyre, from Greenock to Barbados and St Vincent in October 1802. [GA#1/73]

ATLANTIC, Captain Lawson, from Greenock on 4 September 1825 bound for Quebec, arrived there on 11 October 1825; from Aberdeen to Montreal in August 1826, [CCMA: 19.10.1825][NAS.E504.1.32]

AUGUSTA, from Dumfries to New Brunswick in March 1817; master W. Bruce, from Greenock on 19 April 1822, arrived in Quebec on 2 June 1822. [DWJ.18.3.1817][MG:8.6.1822]

AURORA, Captain McLean, from the Clyde on 29 July 1802 bound for Pictou, Nova Scotia; Captain Boyd, from the Clyde to New York 27 September 1802. [GA#1/59, 76]

AURORA, Captain Neilson, from Greenock on 27 July 1824, arrived in Quebec on 8 September 1824. [CC.15.9.1824]

AVON OF LEITH, master Alexander Urquhart, from Leith bound for Charleston, South Carolina, in July 1770. [CM#7534]

BACHELOR OF BOSTON, a brigantine, master Thomas Eyre, from Port Glasgow to Madeira in September 1691. [NAS.E72.15.22]

BACHELOR OF LEITH, master James Mitchell, from Greenock to Virginia on 10 October 1741; arrived in Greenock on 22 May 1742 from Virginia. [CM#3363/3387][NAS.AC9.1476]

BALCLUTHA, from Greenock to Newfoundland in November 1829. [NAS.E504.15.170]

BALFOUR, 150 tons, 8 guns, master David Ballentine, from
Burntisland *with passengers* to Charleston, South Carolina, in
October 1741, sailed 3 November. [CM#3353/3368]

BALTIMORE OF GLASGOW, master William Gemmil, arrived
in Greenock on 7 February 1741 from Virginia; from
Greenock to Virginia on 2 May 1741; arrived in Greenock on
23 January 1742 from Maryland; from Greenock to Virginia
in 17 April 1742; arrived in Port Glasgow on 8 February 1743
from Maryland. [CM#3258/3293/3335/3372]
[NAS.E504.28.1]

BARBADOS MERCHANT, master Robert Williamson, arrived in
Leith on 15 November 1665 from Barbados, [NAS.E72.15.2];
master Cuthbert Sharples, arrived in Port Glasgow in July
1689 from Virginia; arrived in Port Glasgow from Virginia
via Beaumaris, on 12 February 1691; [NAS.E72.19.14/21]

BARBARA OF COLERAINE, master John Baker, arrived in Port
Glasgow on 23 May 1696 from Antigua. [NAS.E72.15.23]

BARBARA, a brig, master J. R. Wilson, arrived in Quebec on 17
May 1818 from Aberdeen; arrived in Quebec on 21 May 1819
from Aberdeen. [MG:2.6.1819]

BEATTIE OF BO'NESS, master John Finlayson, from Greenock
to Antigua in 1712. [NAS.AC8.139]

BECKIE OF GREENOCK, master Colin Campbell, from
Greenock to Jamaica in January 1768. [NAS.E504.15.15]

BEE, master Robert Hasty, from the Clyde to Antigua in 1735.
[GHG#210]

BELLA, from Greenock to New Providence in October 1829.
[NAS.E504.15.170]

BELLE ISLE, Captain Clark, from the Clyde to Jamaica on 5 July
1802. [GA#1/52]

BELLISARIUS, Captain Tibbett, from the Clyde to Boston on 17
September 1802. [GA#1/74]

BENJAMIN OF NEW YORK, master John Laverock, from Leith to Tobago in January 1773. [NAS.E504.22.17]

BENJAMIN OF HONDURAS, a brigantine, arrived in Leith from the Bay of Honduras, 1775. [NAS.AC7.55; AC7.58]

BEN LOMOND, master W. Rattray, arrived in Quebec on 21 July 1820 *with 218 passengers* from Greenock; arrived in Quebec on 3 August 1823 from Grenock. [MG][MH:6.9.1823]

BENSON, Captain Rowe, arrived in Quebec on 27 July 1821 *with 287 passengers* from Greenock. [QM:27.7.1821] [MG:27.6.1821]

BETHIA OF IRVINE, master John Craig, from Irvine, Ayrshire, to Boston in August 1748. [NAS.E504.18.1]

BETSEY, master John Gillies, arrived in the James River, Virginia, on 24 May 1760 from Glasgow, [VG:30.5.1760]; master William Gilkison, from Greenock to St Kitts in April 1763; Master John Gillies, arrived in the James River, Virginia, on 24 May 1766 from Glasgow via Rotterdam, [VaGaz]; master John Gillies, arrived in the James River, Virginia, on 2 February 1767 from Glasgow via Dunkirk, [VaGaz]; master William Dunlop, from Greenock to Antigua in January 1767, [NAS.E504.15.11/14]; master …. McGuffie, arrived in the James River, Virginia, on 11 December 1768 from Glasgow, [VG:22.121.1768]; master James Ramsay, from Port Glasgow to Barbados in May 1776, [NAS.E504.28.26]

BETSY OF LEITH, 150 tons, master Henry Steel, from Leith to Grenada in April 1772, and in February 1773. [NAS.E504.22.17/18/19]

BETSY OF GREENOCK, Captain D. Wither, arrived in Quebec on 15 August 1820 *with 44 passengers* from Oban, Argyll. [QM: 15.8.1820]

BETTY OF PORT GLASGOW, 100 tons, master John Finlayson, from the Clyde via Dublin to Antigua in 1711. [NAS.AC8/139, 168, & AC9/511][NAS.HCA.26/15] [SC:15.3.1711]

BETTY OF GLASGOW, master Robert Simpson, from Greenock to Barbados in January 1717. [NAS.E508.10.6]

BETTY OF GLASGOW, master John Somerville, from Port Glasgow to Jamaica and return, pre 1730, [NAS.AC7.35.354; AC8.415]; master Ninian Bryce, from the Clyde to New England in 1731, [NAS.AC7.43.4; AC9.1425]; master William Dunlop, from the Clyde to Virginia in 1735, arrived in Port Glasgow on 20 December 1735 from Virginia. [GHG#210][NAS.E512/1455]; master William Dunlop, arrived in Hampton, Virginia, in June 1738 from Glasgow; arrived in the James River, Virginia, in 1739 from Glasgow; arrived in Greenock on 18 September 1740 from Virginia; master James Crawford, from Greenock on 17 February 1741 to Virginia; arrived in Greenock on 19 September 1741 from Virginia; master John Gray, from Greenock to Virginia on 23 March 1742; arrived in Port Glasgow on 20 October 1742 from Virginia. [VG#99][VG:4.5.1739] [CM#3197/3262/3355/3361] [NAS.E504.28.1]

BETTY OF LEITH, master Robert Scott later Robert Crawford, from Leith *with passengers* to Virginia in March 1742. [CM#3352/3371]

BETTY OF METHIL, 80 tons, master Robert Salmond, from Kirkcaldy to Boston, New England, in 1754.[NAS.E504.20.3]

BETTY, master John Moor, from Greenock to Jamaica in October 1758; master John Campbell, from Greenock to Jamaica in April 1762; master James Malcolm, from Greenock to Jamaica in December 1762; from Greenock via Jamaica to Virginia in October 1763; from Greenock to Jamaica in November 1764; master Robert Davidson, from Greenock to Jamaica in April 1767. [NAS.E504.15.9/11/12/14]

BETTY, master James Gardner, from Port Glasgow to Newfoundland in August 1776, [NAS.E504.28.26]

BETTY OF PORT GLASGOW, a brigantine, master John Fullarton, from Port Glasgow via Waterford to St Lucia and St Thomas in the West Indies, 1782. [NAS.AC7.64]

BETTY AND JEAN OF IRVINE, master Thomas Glen, from Greenock to Barbados in April 1746. [NAS.E504.15.2]

BETTY AND MARY OF ABERDEEN, master James Melvin, from Aberdeen to Antigua in March 1749; master Lewis Gellie, from Aberdeen to Antigua in February 1750. [NAS.E504.1.3]

BLANDFORD, master Andrew McLarty, from Greenock to Grenada in September 1763, [NAS.E504.15.11/16]

BLESSING OF AYR, from Ayr *with passengers* to Barbados in 1644. [AA.B6.12.9]

BLESSING, from Aberdeen *with passengers* to Philadelphia in 1741.

BLESSING, Captain Watson, arrived in Quebec on 7 June 1818 from Leith. [MG: 17.6.1818]

BOGLE, master Andrew Sym, arrived in the Upper District of the James River, Virginia, on 21 August 1745 from Glasgow via France. [VaGaz#480]

BOLIVAR, from Dundee to Charleston and Savannah in November 1828 and in December 1829. [NAS.E504.11.26]

BON ACCORD OF ABERDEEN, master William Ross, from Aberdeen to Virginia and Maryland pre 1747, wrecked on Barren Island, Chesapeake Bay. [NAS.AC8.689]

BONADVENTURE OF IRVINE, returned to Ayr from the West Indies in 1647.[AA]

BOWMAN, master ...Stevenson, arrived in Hampton, Virginia, in April 1769 from Glasgow. [VG:27.4.1769]

BOYD OF GLASGOW, master William Dunlop, from Greenock on 30 April 1741 to Virginia; from Greenock to Virginia on 1 May 1742; arrived in Port Glasgow on 3 December 1742 from Virginia. [CM#3292/3378][NAS.E504.28.1]

BOYD OF IRVINE, from Ayrshire to Antigua in 1760.
[GA.Shawfield MS#B10/15/6710]

BOYD, arrived in Boston in December 1769 from Glasgow.
[BoNL#3453]

BOYD, Captain Lyon, from Greenock *with passengers* bound for
Wilmington, North Carolina, in January 1802. [GA#4]

BRANDYWINE MILLER, an American brig, master George
Fram, from Greenock *with passengers* to New York in
January 1802, sailed 6 February 1802; master Robert
Dunlevy, from Greenock to New York on 23 August 1802.
[GA#1/8/57]

BREADALBANE, 237 ton brig, master James McFarlane, arrived
in Prince Edward Island on 17 May 1809 from Kirkcaldy,
Fife. [PAPEI/RG9]

BRILLIANT, Captain Barclay, from Aberdeen on 17 August 1823,
arrived in Quebec on 5 October 1823; from Aberdeen on 18
April 1825 bound for Quebec, arrived there on 18 May 1825;
from Aberdeen on 1 April 1826 bound for Quebec, arrived
there on 15 May 1826; from Leith to Quebec in July 1829.
[CCMA:25.5.1825; 20.5.1826]
[CC:11.10.1823][NAS.E504.22.128]

BRITANNIA OF GLASGOW, master Archibald McLarty, from
Greenock to Jamaica in October 1764; from Greenock to
Jamaica in January 1766, and in February 1768.
[NAS.E504.15.12/13/14/15]

BRITANNIA, master William Service, from Greenock to Kingston,
Jamaica, in January 1802, sailed 11 February 1802. [GA#2/9]

BRITANNIA, Captain Cowan, from Greenock to Newfoundland in
February 1802. [GA#14]

BRITANNIA, a brig, from Kirkcudbright to Barbados in 1814;
from Dumfries to Miramichi, New Brunswick, in February
1820. [DWJ: 6.12.1814; 1.2.1820]

BRITISH QUEEN, 191 tons, Captain Denniston, from Greenock to Quebec in 1790. [L]

BRITISH KING, from Dundee to New York in December 1828. [NAS.E504.11.26]

BRITISH TAR, Captain Benson, from Inverkeithing to Jamaica in December 1826. [NAS.E504.16.1]

BROKE, 300 tons, master Dougal Cowan, arrived in Quebec *with 176 passengers* from Greenock, [QM]; Captain McCulloch, from Glasgow *with passengers* bound for New York on 10 July 1823. [DPCA#1091]

BROTHERS OF IRVINE, master Hugh Clark, from Irvine, Ayrshire, to Barbados in March 1747. [NAS.E504.18.1]

BROTHERS OF WHITEHAVEN, arrived in Dumfries on 29 December 1762 from Virginia. [Dumfries Customs Records]

BROTHERS, an American ship, Captain Wickes, from Port Glasgow to Philadelphia in August 1802. [GA#1/58]

BROWN, master Robert Hall, from Greenock to St Kitts in January 1763; master John Cathcart, from Greenock to Jamaica, in September 1767. [NAS.E504.15.11/14]

BRUCE, master Alexander Greig, arrived in Quebec on 13 August 1820 *with 11 passengers* from Aberdeen. [QM]

BRUNSWICK OF LONDONDERRY, a galley, master John Rodger, from Port Glasgow to Jamaica in October 1716, [NAS.E508.10.6]

BRUNSWICK, master ...McLarty, arrived in the James River, Virginia, in March 1772 from Glasgow. [VG:12.3.1772]

BUTTERFLY OF GLASGOW, master Robert Lyon, from Greenock to Barbados in December 1742; also from Greenock to Jamaica in December 1743. [NAS.E504.15.1]

BYRD, master Archibald Bog, from Greenock to Nevis and St Kitts in January 1766. [NAS.E504.15.13]

CAESAR, Captain McMichan, arrived in Quebec on 8 August 1821 *with 55 passengers* from Greenock; from Greenock on 13 April 1822, arrived in Quebec on 4 June 1822. [MG:15.8.1821;8.6.1822]

CALEDONIA, arrived in Dumfries on 20 September 1738 from Virginia or Maryland. [Dumfries Customs Records]

CALEDONIA, master John Fairrie, from Port Glasgow to Jamaica in January 1802, sailed 18 February 1802. [GA#6/14]

CALEDONIA, Captain McGregor, from Aberdeen on 1 April 1825, arrived in Quebec on 18 May 1825; from Aberdeen to Jamaica in April 1826. [CCMA: 25.5.1825][NAS.E504.1.32]

CALEDONIA, from Greenock *with passengers* bound for Philadelphia, arrived there on 11 November 1816, [NARA.M425.23]; master J. Reid, from Greenock bound for Montreal *with 4 passengers,* arrived in Quebec on 14 June 1817, [MG:23.6.1817]; Captain Miller, arrived in Quebec during June 1827 *with 79 passengers* from Greenock; from Irvine to Montreal in August 1828, [NAS.E504.18.20]; arrived in Quebec during June 1829 *with 130 passengers* from Greenock. [QM:2.6.1827/23.6.1829]

CALHOUN OF GLASGOW, master George Douglas, from Port Glasgow to St Kitts in October 1747. [NAS.E504.28.3]

CAMBRIA, a brig, Captain Wilson, arrived in Quebec on 9 September 1817 *with 11 passengers* from Aberdeen.[MG]

CAMILLA, master D. McCarthy, arrived in Quebec on 13 July 1818 *with 109 passengers* from Greenock; master Alexander Harley, from Greenock on 14 April 1819 *with 76 passengers* bound for Quebec, arrived there on 1 June 1819. [MG:23.7.1818; 9.6.1819]

CAMILLUS, a US ship, Captain Peck, from Glasgow *with passengers* bound for New York on 1 August 1823, arrived there on 17 September 1823; from Greenock *with passengers* bound for New York, arrived there on 12 April 1828; from

Greenock *with passengers* bound for New York, arrived there on 3 May 1828. [DPCA#1094][NARA.M237/4, 11, 13]

CANADA, Captain Harvie, from Greenock to Quebec on 22 April 1802. [GA#1/30]

CANADA, Captain Robertson, from Greenock on 15 August 1819, arrived in Quebec on 27 September 1819. [MG.6.10.1819]

CARLTON, from Port Glasgow to Quebec in July 1829. [NAS.E504.28.149]

CAROLINA MERCHANT, master James Gibson, from Glasgow to the Caribee Islands on 29 April 1686. [NAS.E72.19.12]

CASSANDRA, master Alexander McMillan, from Port Glasgow to Jamaica in February 1748; from Port Glasgow to Jamaica in January 1749. [NAS.E504.28.3/4]

CASTLE SEMPLE, master Alexander McCurley, from the Clyde via Cork to St Kitts, landed in Antigua pre 1784. [NAS.AC7.61]

CATHCART OF GREENOCK, to Virginia, 1723; from the Clyde to the Chesapeake, 1724; to Virginia and Maryland, 1728. [NAS.AC9.1014/6398; AC7.28.715; AC7.33.44; AC7.36.17]

CATHERINE OF LONDON, master Edward Thomson, arrived in Dundee on 20 October 1637 from the West Indies. [DA.dsl]

CATHERINE OF WHITEHAVEN, from Greenock to Virginia on 25 November 1715. [GCt#2]; master John Stenhouse, from Greenock to Virginia or Maryland in 1718. [NAS.AC7.26.681; AC9.849]

CATHERINE, master A. Drysdale, arrived in Quebec on 11 August 1821 *with 63 passengers* from Leith. [MG:15.8.1821]

CATHERINE, a brig, Captain Fisher, from Irvine *with 6 passengers* bound for Quebec, arrived there on 5 July 1826; from Irvine, Ayrshire, to Quebec in July 1828. [CCMA:12.7.1826][NAS.E504.18.20]

CATHERINE AND EDWARD, an American ship, from Skye and Tobermory *with passengers* to Wilmington, North Carolina, in August 1811. [Dunvegan Castle Muniments #4/883]

CATO, from Dundee to New Orleans in December 1829. [NAS.E504.11.26]

CENTURION OF WHITEHAVEN, master John Golding, to Virginia in 1712; master Edward Lowis, from Virginia to Glasgow, 1728. [NAS.AC10.120; AC7.34.708]

CERES, master Archibald Greig, from St Kitts to Greenock, 1779-1780. [NAS.AC7.58]

CERES, a brig, master D. Baitt, arrived in Quebec on 18 May 1819 from Aberdeen. [MG:26.5.1819]

CHAMPION OF LEITH, 150 tons, master James Murray, from Leith to Jamaica in April 1769; from Leith via Madeira to Antigua and Kingston, Jamaica, in January 1770, *'housewrights, masons and blacksmiths of good characterill meet with good encouragement'* ; from Leith via Madeira bound for Kingston, Jamaica, in January 1771, *'wanted two housecarpenters and a mason';* from Leith to Jamaica in February 1772, in February 1773, and in March 1774. [NAS.E504.22.15/16/17/18][CM#7404/7598]

CHANCE, Captain McDougall, from the Clyde to Newfoundland in August 1802. [GA#1/68]

CHAPMAN OF LEITH, 130 tons, master James Murray, from Leith to Jamaica in March 1772, and in March 1774. [NAS.E504.22.17]

CHARLES OF BELFAST, master Robert Arthur, arrived in Port Glasgow on 1 September 1691 from Montserrat. [NAS.E72.15.21]

CHARLES OF GLASGOW, master Robert Arthur, arrived in Port Glasgow on 20 March 1691 from the West Indies, from Port Glasgow to the West Indies in April 1691. [NAS.E72.15.22]

CHARLES OF WHITEHAVEN, master Richard Benn, arrived in Greenock in November 1725 from Virginia. [EUL.Laing.490.65]

CHARLES AND LILLIE OF GLASGOW, master David Cunningham, from Port Glasgow to Virginia in December 1748. [NAS.E504.28.4]

CHARLES FORBES, Captain Beveridge, from Inverkeithing to Charleston in October 1826. [NAS.E504.16.1]

CHARMING BETSEY OF LEITH, 70 tons, master James Murray, from Leith to South Carolina in September 1753. [NAS.E504.22.5]

CHARMING BETTY OF ABERDEEN, master Robert Ragg, from Aberdeen to Virginia in 1741. [ACA.APB.3.93]

CHARMING BETTY OF LEITH, 60 tons, master William Rolland, from Leith to New York in March 1753. [NAS.E504.22.5]

CHARMING CLEMENTINA OF PORTSOY, master George Skinner, from Aberdeen to St Kitts in April 1752. [NAS.E504.1.4]

CHARMING JEANIE, master John Bannatyne, from Greenock to Jamaica in November 1764; from Greenock to Jamaica in February 1766. [NAS.E504.15.12/13]

CHARMING LILLY OF GLASGOW, master John Douglas, arrived in Inverness on 9 December 1751 from Virginia. [NAS.E504.17.2]

CHARMING MALLY OF DUBLIN, from Strontian, Argyll, *with passengers* to Jamaica in 1735. [NAS.AC9.1565B]

CHARMING MOLLY OF FORT WILLIAM, from the Clyde to America in 1736. [NAS.NRAS#1279/3]

CHARMING NELLY OF ABERDEEN, master Alexander Harvie, to North America, at Cape Fear in March 1762. [ACA.APB.4]

CHARMING PEGGY, master John Orr, from Ayr to Barbados in December 1748. [NAS.E504.4.1]

CHARLOTTE, Captain Gardiner, from Greenock to Jamaica on 20 February 1802. [GA#14]

CHARMING KATIE OF GREENOCK, master William Pettegrew, from Ayr to Halifax, Nova Scotia, in September 1758. [NAS.E504.4.3]

CHEERFUL, a brig, Captain Beveridge, from Greenock *with 4 passengers* bound for Montreal, arrived at Quebec on 14 June 1817; arrived in Quebec on 18 June 1818 from Leith. [MG:23.6.1817; 24.6.1818]

CHERUB, master A. Stevenson, from Greenock in April 1817 *with 7 passengers* bound for Quebec, arrived there on 1 June 1817; arrived in Quebec on 14 May 1818 *with 10 passengers* from Greenock; master William Raeside, arrived in Quebec on 4 May 1819 from Greenock; from Greenock on 10 August 1819 *with 18 passengers* bound for Quebec, arrived there on 26 September 1819; arrived in Quebec on 12 May 1820 *with 4* passengers from Greenock; arrived in Quebec on 15 May 1821 *with 25 passengers* from Greenock; from Greenock on 25 August 1821 *with 21 passengers* bound for Quebec, arrived there on 1 October 1821; from Greenock on 31 March 1822 *with 13 passengers* bound for Quebec, arrived there on 15 May 1822; from Greenock on 19 August 1822 *with 14 passengers* bound for Quebec, arrived there on 1 October 1822; from Greenock on 5 April 1823 *with 16 passengers* bound for Quebec, arrived there on 15 May 1823; from Greenock on 17 August 1823, arrived in Quebec on 26 September 1823; from Greenock on 7 April 1824 *with 11 passengers* bound for Quebec, arrived there on 31 May 1824; from Greenock on 21 August 1825 *with 5 passengers* bound for Quebec, arrived there on 3 October 1825; Miller, from Greenock *with 12 passengers* bound for Quebec on 17 April 1826, arrived there on 19 May 1826; arrived in Quebec during May 1829 *with 15 passengers* from Greenock. [MG: 9.6.1817; 12.5.1819; 6.10.1819; 23.5.1821;10.10.1821; 29.5.1822; 9.10.1822; 5.6.1824] [QM:12.5.1829]

[CC:21.5.1823; 1.10.1823] [CCMA:21.5.1825; 8.10.1825; 24.5.1826]

CHRISTIAN OF LEITH, 110 tons, master George Watt, from Leith to Annapolis, Maryland, in October 1756. [NAS.E504.22.7]

CHRISTIAN, master ....Brown, arrived in the James River, Virginia, on 8 August 1771 from Bo'ness. [VG:8.8.1771]

CHRISTIE OF ABERDEEN, a brigantine, master Robert Gill, from Aberdeen to Antigua, the Grenades and Jamaica in January 1767; from Aberdeen to Tobago, the Grenades, St Vincent, St Kitts, and Antigua on 24 September 1772; master George Craik, from Aberdeen *with passengers* to Tobago, Grenada and Jamaica on 1 October 1773. [AJ#975/978/990/1282/1287/1341/1356]

CITY OF ABERDEEN, Captain Duthie, from Aberdeen *with 8 passengers* bound for Quebec on 3 April 1826, arrived there on 16 May 1826. [CCMA:20.5.1826]

CLARKSTON, master J. Service, sailed from Greenock on 29 August 1820, and arrived in Quebec on 14 October 1820. [QM]

CLEMENTINE, a schooner, from Dumfries to Jamaica in 1802. [DWJ.23.11.1802]

CLIO, Captain Hopper, from Leith on 8 April 1826 bound for Quebec, arrived there on 22 May 1826. [CCMA:27.5.1826]

CLYDE OF GREENOCK, 70 tons, master John Shannon, from Greenock on 21 March 1741 to Antigua; arrived in Greenock on 17 October 1741 from Antigua; master John McCunn, from Greenock to Barbados on 13 February 1742, [CM#3276/3366/3346][NAS.E504.28.1]; master John McCunn, arrived in Hampton, Virginia, on 4 August 1742 via Antigua. [NA.CO5/1320.R3][VSS#121]

CLYDE, master William Smith, from the Clyde to Boston in 1735. [GHG#210]

CLYDE, master Walter Wright, from Port Glasgow to Jamaica in July 1777, [NAS.E504.28.27]

CLYDE, Captain Sheddan, from the Clyde to Newfoundland 22 September 1802. [GA#1/75]

CLYDE, from Irvine, Ayrshire, to Dalhousie, New Brunswick, in August 1828; from Irvine to Dalhousie in April 1829; from Irvine to New Carlisle, Quebec, in August 1829. [NAS.E504.18.20]

CLYDE RIVER, master Adam McLeish, from Greenock via Cork to Guadaloupe and Barbados in December 1762. [NAS.E504.15.11]

COLUMBIA, Captain Watt from the Clyde to Charleston on 3 July 1802. [GA#1/52]

COLUMBUS, 500 tons, master George Bisset, from Leith to Richibucto, New Brunswick, in July 1822; from Dundee to Miramachi on 4 August 1823, [EEC#17,326][DPCA#1097]

COMET, a brig, Captain Leisk, arrived in Quebec on 19 May 1818 from Aberdeen. [MG]

COMMERCE OF GREENOCK, Captain Loudon, from Greenock on 28 July 1804 to Oban, Argyll, from there *with 42 passengers* bound for Quebec in 1804, arrived on 4 September 1804; from Greenock *with passengers* bound for New York, arrived there on 17 July 1823; master N. Coverdale, arrived in Quebec on 5 August 1820 *with 402 passengers* from Greenock on 21 June 1820; from Greenock on 10 May 1821 *with 422 passengers* bound for Quebec, arrived there on 20 June 1821; from Greenock on 4 April 1823 *with 90 passengers* to settle in Marietta, Ohio, arrived in New York on 15 July 1823; Captain Wittleton, arrived in Quebec on 15 September 1824 *with 15 passengers* from Greenock on 1 August 1824. [NAS.GD202.70.11/12][NARA.M237/4] [CC:19.7.1823; CC15.9.1824][QM:28.9.1824][MG:27.6.1821]

CONCORD OF QUEENSFERRY, 150 tons, from the Forth to Virginia in 1711. [SC: 13.4.1711]

CONCORD OF GLASGOW, master Robert Smith, from Port Glasgow to Barbados in November 1713; from Greenock to Antigua in September 1714, [NAS.E508.7.6; E508.8.6]

CONCORD, master Patrick Spink, from Montrose to Virginia in March 1740, arrived in Arbroath from Virginia on 24 November 1740. [NAS.CE53.1.3]

CONCORD, master Alexander Ramage, from Leith in December 1770 bound for Grenada. [CM#7598]

CONCORD OF LEITH, 70 tons, master Mungo Graham, from Leith to Grenada in February 1771. [NAS.E504.22.16]

CONCORD, Captain Guadin, from the Clyde to Newfoundland in August 1802. [GA.1/64]

CONESTOGA, from Greenock *with passengers* bound for Philadelphia, arrived there on 23 October 1820. [NARA.M425.30]

CONFIRMATION OF WHITEHAVEN, master Robert Jackson, from Greenock to Barbados in October 1716; from the Clyde to the West Indies and America, probably Virginia, in 1717. [NAS.E508.10.6; AC7.24.710; AC9.691]

CONVENOR, master Robert Dickie, from Leith to Virginia on 1 July 1740. [CM#5276]

CORSAIR OF GREENOCK, Captain McAlpine, arrived in Quebec on 1 June 1824 from Greenock; arrived in Quebec during September 1825 *with 30 passengers* from Greenock; Captain Hamilton, arrived in Quebec during September 1829 *with 38 passengers* from Greenock. [MG:9.6.1824][QM:20.9.1825/ 8.9.1829]

COUNTESS OF CRAWFORD, Captain Anstruther, from Greenock to Newfoundland on 19 May 1802. [GA#1/39]

COUNTESS OF DARLINGTON, master David Wilson, from Greenock to Montreal in March 1802, sailed 14 April 1802. [GA#20/29]

COUNTESS OF GALLOWAY, a brigantine, from Creetown, Kirkcudbright, to Kingston, Jamaica, on 15 March 1793.

COUNTESS OF MORTON OF ABERDOUR/BURNTISLAND, 110 tons, master George Hunter, from Leith to Grenada in April 1769; from Leith to Grenada in October 1770; master James Orrock, from Kirkcaldy, Fife, to Grenada in March 1772, [NAS.E504.22.15/16; E504.20.8][CM#7567]

CRAWFORD OF GLASGOW, master Robert Lees, arrived in Greenock on 4 March 1743 from Boston; from Greenock to St Kitts in October 1758. [NAS.E504.15.1/9]

CRESCENT, Captain Dunlop, from Greenock to Trinidad on 10 February 1802. [GA#9]

CROWE ISLE, Captain Campbell, from the Clyde to Charleston in August 1802. [GA#1/64]

CULLODEN, a brig, Captain Leyden, arrived in Quebec on 4 June 1824 from Aberdeen; arrived in Quebec on 26 May 1825 from Leith. [MG.9.6.1824] [CMA: 1.6.1825]

CUMBERLAND OF FRASERBURGH, 50 tons, master Andrew Garioch, from Aberdeen to Antigua 14 March 1747. [NAS.E504.1.2]

CURLEW, master J. Young, arrived in Quebec on 9 September 1818 *with 205 passengers* from Greenock; from Greenock *with passengers* to New York, arrived there on 19 July 1828. [MG][QM: 10.9.1818][NARA.M237/12]

CYGNET, a brig, Captain Henderson, arrived in Quebec on 25 May 1820 *with 12 passengers* from Dundee; Captain Murphy, from Greenock on 19 May 1825, arrived in Quebec on 2 July 1825. [QM][CCMA: 2.7.1825]

CYRUS, from Fort William, Inverness-shire, *with passengers* to Pictou, Nova Scotia, in June 1818. [IC.29]

CYRUS OF GLASGOW, master Andrew Robertson, from Leith to Richibucto, New Brunswick, in July 1822, [EEC#17,322];

Captain Richardson, from Leith to Pictou, Nova Scotia, on 31 March 1823. [LCL#XI.1051]

DALMARNOCK, Captain Kinninmont, from Alloa, Clackmannanshire, and Leith *with 9 passengers* to New York on 7 March 1823. [LCL.XI.1054]

DALRYMPLE OF GLASGOW, master Robert Cobham, from Greenock on 17 February 1741 to Virginia; arrived in Greenock on 26 September 1741 from Virginia. [CM#3262/3359]

DANIEL OF CAMPBELTOWN, master John Boyd, from Campbeltown, Argyll, to Barbados on 20 April 1756. [NAS.E504.8.2]

DAPHNE, Captain Wilkie, from Greenock to Newfoundland on 13 March 1802. [GA#20]

DART, Captain Wyllie, from Greenock to Grenada on 18 May 1802. [GA#1/39]

DAVID, Captain Gemmell, arrived in Quebec on 25 June 1821 *with 364 passengers* from Greenock. [MG:27.6.1821]

DEFENCE, from Leith to Miramachi, New Brunswick, in August 1829. [NAS.E504.22.128]

DELIGHT OF DUNDEE, master Alexander Ogilvie, from Montrose, Angus, to Virginia 11 February 1750; from Dundee and Montrose to the Potomac River on 12 June 1751. [NAS.E504.24.2][NAS.RD211.2.107]

DIADEM, a brig, Captain Barclay, from Aberdeen on 24 July 1824, *with 1 passenger* arrived in Quebec on 10 September 1824; from Aberdeen on 26 March 1825 *with passengers* bound for Quebec, arrived there on 13 May 1825; from Aberdeen on 25 July 1825 bound for Quebec, arrived there on 16 September 1825. [CCMA: 15.9.1824; 18.5.1825; 21.9.1825]

DIAMOND, master Robert Arthur, from the Clyde to Virginia in 1735. [GHG#210]; master James Weir, from the Chesapeake via Fort William to the Clyde, 1738. [NAS.AC7.44.488]

DIAMOND OF GLASGOW, master John Easdale, from Greenock to Virginia on 25 July 1741; arrived in Greenock on 29 May 1742 from Virginia. [CM#3332/3391]

DIAMOND, master Thomas Ritchie, arrived in the James River, Virginia, on 23 August 1768 from Glasgow. [VG:1.9.1768]

DIANA, master William Montgomery, from Greenock to Newfoundland in May 1767. [NAS.E504.15.14]

DIANA, Captain Campbell, from Greenock to St Vincent on 10 February 1802, sailed 16 March 1802, also on 14 May 1802 from Greenock to Charlestown; Captain Dyett, from the Clyde to Trinidad in August 1802; from Port Glasgow to St Vincent, Curacao and Grenada *"wanted to serve in the West Indies under indenture for three years, 2 house carpenters, 2 masons and 1 overseer"* [GA#9/20/37/64/74]

DIANA, Captain Fyfe, from Dundee to Miramachi in October 1822; from Dundee to Miramachi on 4 August 1823; from Dundee to Miramachi on 1 April 1824. [NAS.E504.11.23][DPCA#1097/1132]

DIANA, from Dumfries to St John, New Brunswick, on 1 April 1829; master William Lookup, from Dumfries to Dalhousie, New Brunswick, on 5 July 1829. [NAS.E504.9.10]

DILIGENCE OF GLASGOW, master John Lyon, arrived in Glasgow on 3 January 1735 from Virginia. [EUL.Laing.490.121]

DILIGENCE OF ABERDEEN, 100 tons, master George Duncan, from Aberdeen to Maryland, 1750; from Aberdeen to Antigua in March 1752. [NAS.AC9.1748; E504.1.4]

DILIGENCE, master R. Kirk, arrived in Quebec on 13 August 1820 *with 10 passengers* from Leith. [QM]

DISPATCH OF NEWCASTLE, master Alexander Thistlewait, from Aberdeen to Virginia in May 1749. [NAS.E504.1.3]

DOLPHIN OF BOSTON, a pink, master Alexander McCall, arrived in Glasgow on 20 July 1686 from Virginia; from Glasgow on 30 August 1686 bound for Madeira. [NAS.E72.19.12]

DOLPHIN OF BOSTON, arrived in Inverness from America in May 1711. [SC: 26.5.1711]

DOLPHIN OF DUNDEE, master George Glas, from Perth to Jamaica and the Leeward Islands, 28 February 1752; from Dundee to Jamaica in November 1753; arrived in Dundee on 10 May 1755 from the Canary Islands. [NAS.E504.27.2; E504.11.3]

DOVE OF GREENOCK, master Samuel Cuthbert, from Greenock on 8 January 1741 to Antigua; arrived in Greenock on 22 August 1741 from Antigua. [CM#3244/3344]; master William Hyndman, arrived in Greenock on 28 October 1742 from Virginia; from Greenock on 29 January 1743 to St Kitts and Barbados; master William Sempill, from Port Glasgow to Jamaica in October 1744; from Port Glasgow to Antigua in September 1743. [NAS.E504.15.1; E504.28.1/2; CS96.1920]

DOVE OF GLASGOW, a snow, master John Andrews, from Glasgow on 30 October 1739, arrived in the James River, Virginia, in January 1740; master William Sempill, from Port Glasgow in September 1743 to Antigua; from Port Glasgow to Jamaica in August 1745; from Port Glasgow to St Kitts in December 1747; from Port Glasgow to Jamaica in January 1749. [VaGaz#181][NAS.E504.28.1/2/3/4]

DRAGON OF LONDON, master Alexander Lawson, from Aberdeen to Jamaica on 13 November 1746. [NAS.E504.1.2]

DRAPER, an American ship, master Ormond Noble, from Greenock to New York in April 1802. [GA#1/26]

DRUMMOND OF GLASGOW, from Glasgow to Virginia, Jamaica, Barbados, and return to Inverness in 1722. [NAS.AC7.8.285]

DUCHESS OF RICHMOND, Captain Cook, arrived in Quebec on 17 August 1820 *with 266 passengers* from Oban; arrived in

Quebec on 4 August 1821 *with 266 passengers* from
Greenock; Captain Cunningham, from Greenock on 13
August 1823, arrived in Quebec on 29 September 1823;
Captain McGlashan, from Greenock on 7 August 1824 *with
20 passengers* bound for Quebec, arrived there on 26
September 1824. [QM][MG:15.8.1821][CC.4.10.1823;
2.10.1824]

DUKE OF ATHOLL, master Robert Grindlay, from Bo'ness to
Charleston, South Carolina, in August 1770. [CM#7536]

DUNLOP, master John Heartwell, from Port Glasgow to Quebec in
April 1776, [NAS.E504.28.26]

DUNLOP, master Allan Stevenson, arrived in Quebec during June
1810 *with 54 passengers* from Glasgow. [QGaz: 14.6.1810]

DUNLOP, Captain Mundell, from Greenock *with 220 passengers*
bound for Canada, 96 landed at Sydney, Cape Breton, and 134
at Quebec on 30 August 1824. [CC.4.9.1824]

DWINA, a brig, master Thomas Thompson, from Peterhead on 1
May 1822, arrived in Quebec on 23 June 1822; from
Peterhead on 22 May 1823, arrived in Quebec on 15 July
1823; from Peterhead on 17 April 1824, arrived in Quebec on
3 June 1824; Captain Yule, from Peterhead on 20 April 1826
bound for Quebec, arrived there on 30 May 1826.
[MG:29.6.1822; 9.6.1824][CC:19.7.1823][CCMA:3.6.1826]

EAGLE, master James Ewing, arrived in Hampton, Virginia, during
May 1766 from Glasgow. [VG]

EAGLE, Captain Connolly, from Greenock to Quebec in April
1802, sailed on 16 June 1802; arrived in Quebec during
September 1802 from Greenock *with 21 passengers*.
[GA#17/47][QGaz 11.9.1802]

EAGLE, master William Morrison, from Greenock to Norfolk,
Virginia, in March 1802. [GA#19]

EARL OF BUCKINGHAMSHIRE, 593 tons, Captain Johnson,
from Greenock *with 160 passengers* on 28 May 1822, arrived
in Quebec on 5 July 1822. [MG:10.7.1822]

EARL OF DALHOUSIE, a brig, master J. Livie, arrived in Quebec on 12 May 1818 *with 14 passengers* from Aberdeen; arrived in Quebec on 12 May 1819 *with 24 passengers* from Aberdeen; master Thomas Johnson, arrived in Quebec on 24 June 1820 *with 200 passengers* from Greenock; arrived in Quebec on 15 May 1821 *with 15 passengers* from Aberdeen; Captain Boyd, arrived in Quebec during October 1827 *with 20 passengers* from Greenock. [MG.19.5.1819; 23.5.1821][QM: 9.10.1827]

ECLIPSE, a brig, Captain Moore, arrived in Quebec on 2 June 1818 *with 10 passengers* from Greenock; arrived in Quebec on 2 June 1824 from Ayr; from Troon on 18 April 1825, arrived in Quebec on 26 May 1825; arrived in Quebec on 8 July 1826 from Ayr; from Ayr to Chaleur Bay in February 1827, from Ayr to Dalhousie, New Brunswick, in April 1829. [MG:10.6.1818; 9.6.1824][CCMA:1.6.1825; 15.7.1826] [NAS.E504.4.15]

ECONOMY, Captain Balfour, from Dundee to Miramachi on 1 April 1824. [DPCA#1132]

EDINBURGH, 100 tons, master Ninian Bryce, from Leith to Jamaica in February 1749; master Samuel Swinton, from Leith to Jamaica in March 1750. [NAS.E504.22.3]

EDINBURGH, a brigantine, master Robert Alexander, was condemned by the Vice Admiralty Court at New Providence, the Bahamas, on 5 February 1770; from Leith in July 1770 bound for Charleston, South Carolina, *'two house carpenters and two tailors are wanted'.* [ActsPCCol.1770/162][CM#7533]

EDWARD OF LEITH, 360 tons, master John Smith, from Leith to Philadelphia, Norfolk, Petersburg, and Richmond, Virginia, in April 1822, *'any passenger going by way of Washington and Baltimore will find this an opportunity'*, [EEC#17,260]; from Leith *with 32 passengers* to Philadelphia on 15 April 1823. [LCL.X.932]

EGLINTON OF SALTCOATS, master William Dunlop, from Greenock on 21 March 1741 to Virginia; arrived in Greenock on 24 October 1741 from Virginia, [CM#3276/3368]; master Henry Scott, from Irvine, Ayrshire, to Virginia in August 1745. [NAS.E504.18.1]

EGLINTON, master William Hamilton, from Port Glasgow to Boston, New England, in August 1802. [GA#1/63]

ELEANOR, Captain Bell, from Greenock on 6 August 1821 *with 2 passengers* bound for Quebec, arrived there on 14 September 1821. [MG:26.9.1821]

ELIZA OF GLASGOW, a snow, master Daniel Clark, from Greenock to Virginia on 12 May 1741; arrived in Greenock on 28 November 1741 from Virginia; arrived in Greenock on 19 February 1743 from Virginia; master David Blair, from Port Glasgow to the Isle of May (Isle of Maia, Cape Verde Islands), and Virginia in February 1745, arrived in the York River, Virginia, on 25 June 1745; from Port Glasgow to the Isle of May in January 1746.
[CM#3299/3313][NAS.E504.15.1; E504.28.2][VaGaz#466]

ELIZA, master Robert Jack, from Port Glasgow to Quebec in March 1777. [NAS.E504.28.27]

ELIZA, Captain McAllister, from Greenock to Pictou, Nova Scotia, in April 1802. [GA#1/30]

ELIZA, Captain Burgess, from Inverkeithing to New York in September 1822. [NAS.E504.16.1]

ELIZA, Captain Duthie, from Peterhead on 13 April 1823, arrived in Quebec on 22 May 1823. [CC:228.5.1823]

ELIZA, a 257 ton brig, master George Hynd, from Dundee to New York in October 1824; from Dundee to New York in September 1829. [DPCA#1159][NAS.E504.11.26]

ELIZA ANN, master A.Grierson, arrived in Quebec on 15 July 1819 *with 47 passengers* from Greenock. [MG:21.7.1819]

ELIZABETH OF GLASGOW, master James Campbell, from Port Glasgow to the Canary Islands in December 1690. [NAS.E72.19.22]

ELIZABETH, master Thomas Shadwick, arrived in Port Glasgow on 2 June 1691 from Virginia. [NAS.E72.15.21]

ELIZABETH OF GLASGOW, 160 tons, from the Clyde to Barbados in 1711. [SC: 12.9.1711]

ELIZABETH OF ABERDEEN, master William Dun, to the West Indies in 1720. [NAS.AC9.709]

ELIZABETH OF GLASGOW, master Daniel Clark, from Greenock to South Carolina on 4 October 1740; master William Hyndman, from Port Glasgow to St Kitts in July 1745. [CM#3204][NAS.E504.28.2]

ELIZABETH OF GREENOCK, master James Heasty, arrived at Rothesay, Bute, on 31 January 1741 from St Kitts; from Greenock via Belfast and the Isle of Maia to Carolina on 17 October 1741; master William Orr, from Greenock to Jamaica in October 1744; master Robert Ramsay, from Greenock to St Kitts in March 1746. [CM#3255/3366][NAS.E504.15.2]

ELIZABETH, master Andrew Geils, arrived in Hampton, Virginia, during May 1745 from Glasgow. [VG#460]

ELIZABETH OF GLASGOW, master James Heasty, from Stranraer, Wigtownshire, to Virginia on 10 September 1746. [NAS.E504.34.1]

ELIZABETH OF VIRGINIA, master Alexander Leslie, arrived in Montrose on 30 August 1748 from Rappahannock, Virginia. [NAS.CE53.1.4]

ELIZABETH, master .....Kerr, arrived in the James River, Virginia, on 11 December 1768 from Glasgow. [VG:22.12.1768]

ELIZABETH OF DUNDEE, 100 tons, master Andrew Peddie, from Dundee via Rotterdam and Madeira to Savannah-la-Mar, Jamaica in December 1775. [NAS.E504.11.9]

ELIZABETH, master Robert Raside, from Greenock to Jamaica in January 1802. [GA#2]

ELIZABETH OF BOSTON, Captain Burgess, from Dundee to New York in January 1822. [NAS.E504.11.23]

ELIZABETH, Captain Grayson, from Greenock on 28 July 1825, arrived in Quebec on 8 September 1825. [CCMA: 14.9.1825]

ELIZABETH AND PEGGY OF LEITH, master Walter Scott, from Leith to South Carolina in May 1753. [NAS.E504.22.5]

ELIZABETH AND THOMAS OF GREENOCK, a brigantine, master Thomas Adair, from Maryland to Glasgow, 1787. [NAS.AC7.63]

ELLEN, Captain King, from Aberdeen on 23 June 1822 *with 1 passenger* bound for Quebec, arrived there on 5 September 1822. [MG:11.9.1822]

EMERALD, a brig, Captain Leslie, from Greenock on 12 April 1826 bound for Quebec, arrived there on 19 May 1826. [CCMA:24.5.1826]

EMPEROR ALEXANDER OF ABERDEEN, master A. Watts, arrived in Quebec on 22 October 1823 *with 49 passengers* from Tobermory, Mull, on 23 July 1823; arrived in Quebec on 4 June 1824 from Aberdeen. [QM:7.10.1823][CC:11.10.1823] [MG:9.6.1824]

ENDEAVOUR OF CHARLESTOWN, NEW ENGLAND, master John Brakenbury, from Port Glasgow to the West Indies in November 1688; arrived in Port Glasgow on 20 July 1689 from Nevis; from Port Glasgow to Madeira in September 1689. [NAS.E72.19.14/15]

ENDEAVOUR OF GLASGOW, master Peter Hunckin, arrived in Port Glasgow on 24 August 1691 from New England. [NAS.E72.15.21]

ENDEAVOUR OF IRVINE, 100 tons, arrived in Irvine, Ayrshire, from South Carolina in 1711. [SC:4.12.1711]

ENDEAVOUR OF LEITH, 70 tons, master William Watson, from Leith to South Carolina in July 1753, also in September 1754, and in September 1755. [NAS.E504.22.5/6]

ENDYMION, Captain Miller, from Port Glasgow to Virginia in April 1802. [GA#1/28]; master Edward Todd, from Grangemouth on 8 April 1819, arrived in Quebec on 12 May 1819. [MG:19.5.1819]

ENTERPRISE, Captain Patton, arrived in Quebec on 25 May 1820 *with 39 passengers* from Ayr. [QM: 25.5.1820]; Captain Hunter, from Ayr to the Bay of Chaleur in April 1825, and from Ayr to Restigouche, Canada, in July 1826. [NAS.E504.4.15]

EUNICE, from Glasgow *with passengers* bound for New York, arrived there on 13 December 1827. [NARA,M237.11]

EUPHEMIA OF GLASGOW, 70 tons, master Jonathan Bowman, arrived in the Rappahannock River, Virginia, on 7 December 1725 from Glasgow via Barbados. [VSS#54/55]

EUPHEMIA, master James Lyon, to Charleston, 1731. [NAS.AC9.6455]

EUPHRATES, Captain Galt, from Greenock to Jamaica on 16 February 1802. [GA#13]

EUROPA, Captain McArthur, from Port Glasgow to Nevis in May 1802. [GA#1/41]

EWE AND LAMB, master John Guthrie, from Leith on 4 January 1667 bound for Virginia. [NAS.E72.15.6]

EXPEDITION OF GLASGOW, a 100 ton galley, from Virginia to the Clyde in 1711; master Duncan Campbell, from Greenock to Jamaica in October 1713 and in October 1714; master William Dunlop, from Port Glasgow to Jamaica in November 1716. [SC:23.6.1711][NAS.E508.7.6; E508.8.6]

EXPEDITION, a schooner, from Peterhead on 19 April 1824, arrived in Quebec on 2 June 1824; Captain Watson, from Aberdeen to Jamaica in April 1826. [MG.9.6.1824][NAS.E504.1.32]

EVANS OF BURNTISLAND, 90 tons, master John Cordis, from Kirkcaldy, Fife, to Antigua in February 1775. [NAS.E504.20.8]

EXPEDITION OF INVERKEITHING, 150 tons, master David Ingles, from Leith to Grenada, in May 1765. [NAS.E504.22.12]

FACTOR, a 300 ton American ship, master Josiah F. Caldwell, from Greenock to New York in October 1802. [GA#1/74]

FAIRFIELD, Captain Morris, from Aberdeen in April 1817 *with 12 passengers* bound for Quebec, arrived there on 1 June 1817. [MG: 9.6.1817]

FALMOUTH, master David Starret, from Port Glasgow to Halifax, Nova Scotia, in March 1777. [NAS.E504.28.27]

FAME OF LIVERPOOL, master John Glover, arrived in Glasgow on 2 March 1689 from Virginia. [NAS.E72.19.14]

FAME OF GLASGOW, master James Hume, arrived in Port Glasgow during February 1735 from Maryland. [NAS.E512/1455]

FAME OF AYR, from Ayr to Newfoundland in April 1765. [NAS.E504.4.3]

FAME, a brig, master Robert Reid, from Greenock to Trinidad in January 1802, sailed 6 May 1802. [GA#2/35]

FAME, a brig, Captain Abrams, from Greenock on 12 April 1818 *with passengers* bound for Quebec, arrived there on 18 May 1818; Captain Malcolm, from Leith on 12 June 1824 *with 113passengers* bound for Quebec, arrived there on 30 July 1824; from Greenock in April 1826 bound for Quebec, arrived there on 23 May 1826.[MG] [CCMA:27.5.1826]

FAME, master George Masson, arrived in Quebec on 2 September 1819 from Aberdeen. [MG:15.9.1819]

FANNY, master William Robertson, from Port Glasgow to Antigua in July 1777. [NAS.E504.28.27]

FANNY, master Daniel H. Braine, from Greenock to New York in March 1802. [GA#9]

FAVOURITE, Captain Boag, from Greenock to Quebec in February 1802, sailed 4 April 1802. [GA#9/26]

FAVOURITE OF ST JOHN, NEW BRUNSWICK, 391 tons, master John Hyndman, from port Glasgow on 22 October 1815 *with 133 passengers* bound for St John, NB.[PANB]

FAVOURITE OF MONTREAL, a brig, Captain Grey, arrived in Quebec on 16 July 1818 *with 23 passengers* from Greenock; master Alexander Allan, from Greenock *with 12 passengers* bound for Quebec on 27 August 1825, arrived there on 11 October 1825; from Greenock *with 15 passengers* bound for Quebec and Montreal on 12 April 1826, arrived in Quebec on 17 May 1826 and in Montreal on 21 May 1826; arrived in Quebec during October 1826 *with 79 passengers* from Greenock; arrived in Quebec during September 1829 *with 40 passengers* from Greenock. [MG:1.7.1818] [QM: 14.10.1826/29.9.1829] [CCMA:19.10.1825; 24.5.1826]

FAVOURITE, Captain Gray, from Ayr to Pictou, Nova Scotia, in April 1824. [NAS.E504.4.15]

FINLAYS, master Hugh Coulter, from Greenock via Dublin to Barbados in November 1758. [NAS.E504.15.9]

FISHER AND FRIENDSHIP OF LEITH, 120 tons, master William Forrester, from Leith to Grenada in April 1771; from Leith to Grenada in February 1772. [NAS.E504.22.16/17]

FLORA, master J. Work, arrived in Quebec on 16 May 1818 *with 3 passengers* from Aberdeen. [MG]

FORLORN OF GLASGOW, master William Eccles, from Greenock to Barbados in January 1716, [NAS.E508.9.6]

FORTH OF LEITH, 130 tons, master Robert Brown, from Leith to Virginia in June 1754. [NAS.E504.22.6]

FORTH, arrived in Quebec during July 1827 *with 150 passengers* from Greenock. [QM:17.7.1827]

FORTUNE OF GLASGOW, master James Campbell, from Port Glasgow to the Canary Islands in April 1690; master Robert Arthur, from Port Glasgow to Barbados in October 1713; master James Porter, from Virginia to Glasgow, 1729 [NAS.E72.19.22; E508.7.6; AC9.1085]

FOUNDLING, Captain McLeod, arrived in Quebec during July 1829 *with 170 passengers* from Greenock. [QM:1.8.1829]

FRANCES, Captain Patterson, arrived in Charleston on 11 March 1823 from Dundee. [DPCA#1082]

FREEMASON OF GOUROCK, later OF GLASGOW master John McCun, from Greenock on 4 April 1741 to Virginia; from Greenock to Virginia on 20 February 1742. [CM#3282/3350]

FRIENDS, master Duncan McFarlane, from Port Glasgow to Dominica in August 1776, [NAS.E504.28.26]

FRIENDS, a brig, from Kirkcudbright to Nova Scotia in May 1801. [DWJ.5.5.1801]

FRIENDS, Captain Johnston, from Greenock to New Brunswick in April 1802. [GA#1/30]

FRIENDS OF SALTCOATS, master John How, arrived in Quebec during September 1802 *with passengers* from Fort William. [QGaz: 15.9.1802]

FRIENDS, a brig, Captain Soutar, arrived in Quebec on 21 June 1818 from Peterhead; master W. Soutar, arrived in Quebec on 19 July 1820 from Peterhead; from Peterhead on 26 April 1824, arrived in Quebec on 12 June 1824. [MG:1.7.1818][CC.16.6.1824]

FRIENDS, from Greenock *with passengers* bound for New York, arrived there on 10 May 1823; from Greenock *with passengers* bound for New York, arrived there on 12 May 1826. [NARA.M237.4, 8]

FRIENDS ADVENTURE OF GLASGOW, master Mark Hawking, arrived in Glasgow on 7 September 1686 from Virginia; from Glasgow to New England in October 1686. [NAS.E72.19.12]

FRIENDS ADVENTURE OF LEITH, master David Scott, from Leith to the Chesapeake and return in 1708. [NAS.AC10.88]

FRIENDS GOODWILL OF LEITH, 120 ton, master John Thomson, from Leith to Grenada in January 1770; master John Cready, from Leith to Tobago and Grenada in February 1771. [NAS.E504.22.15/16][CM#7404]

FRIENDSHIP OF BOSTON, a brigantine, master Thomas Eyre, arrived in Port Glasgow on 15 August 1691 from America. [NAS.E72.19.21]

FRIENDSHIP OF LEITH, 130 tons, master Archibald Galbreath, from Leith to Virginia in December 1709. [NAS.E508.4.6]; from Leith to Virginia and Maryland in 1711. [NAS.AC8.114] [SC: 16.8.1711]; master Walter Fleeth, arrived in the Lower James River, Virginia, on 10 January 1716 from Scotland. [NA.CO5.1320/R3; VSS#25]

FRIENDSHIP OF AYR, master John Aitken arrived in Ayr on 30 July 1740 from Virginia; arrived in Ayr in June 1742 from Virginia; from Ayr via Africa to the West Indies in 1744. [CM#3176/3394][NAS.AC8.653]

FRIENDSHIP OF GLASGOW, master Andrew Gray, arrived in Greenock on 27 December 1740 from Virginia; from Greenock to Virginia on 30 April 1741; arrived in Greenock on 12 December 1741 from Virginia; master John Shannon, from Greenock to Virginia on 1 May 1742; arrived in Port Glasgow on 27 November 1742 from Virginia; master John Somerville, arrived in the Upper District of the James River, Virginia, on 24 June 1745 from Glasgow. [CM#3240/3292/3318/3378][NAS.E504.28.1][VaGaz#466]

FRIENDSHIP OF CELLARDYKE, 80 tons, master Andrew Reid, from Leith to Grenada in January 1772, in November 1772, in

November 1773, and in September 1774.
[NAS.E504.22.17/18/19]

FRIENDSHIP OF PHILADELPHIA, 120 tons, master Thomas
Jann, from Leith on 6 May 1775 bound for Philadelphia.
[NAS.E504.22.19]

GALATE, from Greenock *with passengers* bound for New Orleans,
arrived there on 1 September 1827. [NARA.M259.7]

GENERAL GOLDIE, a schooner, master W. Smith, from
Dumfries *with 18 passengers* to Canada in July 1817, arrived
at Quebec on 14 September 1817; from Dumfries *with 30
passengers* bound for Quebec in June 1818.
[DWJ.3.6.1817][NAS.E504.9.9][QM: 16.9.1817][MG]

GENERAL GRAHAM, Captain Alexander, from Leith *with 18
passengers* to Miramichi, New Brunswick, on 8 April 1824.
[LCL.XII.1158]

GENERAL WOLFE, Captain Johnston, from Greenock on 20 July
1825 *with 4 passengers* bound for Quebec, arrived there on
12 September 1825; arrived in Quebec on 19 May 1826 *with
32 passengers* from Greenock on 7 April 1826. [QM:
20.5.1826][CCMA:17.9.1825; 24.5.1826]

GEORGE GALLEY OF GLASGOW, master David Buckling,
arrived in the Potomac River between 1710 and 1718 via
Barbados. [VSS#35]

GEORGE, master John Bell, from Stranraer, Wigtownshire, to
Antigua on 11 February 1767, returned to Stranraer on 1
August 1767. [NAS.E504.34.5]

GEORGE, master Peter Paterson, arrived in the James River,
Virginia, on 29 August 1768 from Aberdeen. [VG:1.9.1768]

GEORGE, master ....Coats, arrived in the James River, Virginia,
in April 1769 from Glasgow. [VG:27.4.1769]

GEORGE OF LEITH, 200 tons, master Philip Welsh, from Leith
to Antigua in November 1769; master Alexander Alexander,

from Leith to Charleston, South Carolina, in November 1770. [NAS.E504.22.15][CM#7567]

GEORGE, master Donald Campbell, from Greenock *with passengers* to New York in February 1802. [GA#5]

GEORGE, master Robert Consitt, arrived in Quebec on 7 September 1819 from Glasgow. [MG:7.9.1819]

GEORGE, master J. McAlpine, from Greenock on 16 June 1822 *with 42 passengers* bound for Quebec, arrived there on 10 August 1822. [MG: 17.8.1822]

GEORGE AND MARY OF BOSTON, master James Cunningham, from Greenock on 12 March 1741 to Boston; arrived in Greenock on 17 October 1741 from Virginia. [CM#3273/3366]

GEORGE AND WILLIAM, master Thomas Warden, from Leith to Jamaica in November 1779. [NAS.E504.22.23]

GEORGE CANNING, Captain Potter, arrived in Quebec on 2 June 1821 *with 489 passengers* from Greenock; Captain Stephen, from Aberdeen on 10 August 1824, arrived in Quebec on 26 September 1824; from Aberdeen to Quebec in August 1827; Captain Callendar, arrived in Montreal during June 1828 *with 180 passengers* from Greenock; arrived in Quebec during May 1829 *with 103 passengers* from Greenock. [MG.13.6.1821][NAS.E504.1.32] [CC.2.10.1824] [QM: 24.6.1828/ 23.5.1829]

GEORGE STEWART, Captain Stewart, from Greenock on 27 May 1825 *with 57 passengers* bound for Quebec, arrived there on 14 July 1825. [QM:16.7.1825][CCMA: 20.7.1825]

GLASGOW MERCHANT, Captain Dredan, arrived in Glasgow on 20 October 1670 from Nevis. [NAS.E72.10.3]

GLASGOW OF GLASGOW, master Andrew Gray, from the Clyde to Virginia in 1735, arrived in Port Glasgow on 3 February 1736 from Virginia; master Andrew Gray, from the Upper District of the James River, Virginia, to Glasgow on 8 September 1736; arrived in the Upper District, James River,

Virginia, from Glasgow via Cadiz on 2 June 1737; master Walter Stirling, arrived in Philadelphia, Pennsylvania, before 1739; master David Blair, arrived in Greenock on 16 May 1741 from Virginia. [VaGaz#7/44] [GHG#210] [NAS.AC8/584; E512/1455][CM#3300]

GLASGOW PACKET OF GREENOCK, master Thomas Watson, from Greenock to Antigua on 17 January 1741; from Greenock to Barbados on 12 December 1741. [CM #3249/3318]

GLASGOW OF ST KITTS, master Thomas Marshall, from Greenock to St Kitts in June 1742. [NAS.E504.15.1]

GLASGOW OF PORT GLASGOW, master John Somerville, from Greenock via the Isle of Maia to Virginia on 9 January 1742; arrived in Port Glasgow on 4 February 1743 from Maryland. [CM#3329][NAS.E504.28.1]

GLASGOW, master Alexander Smith, from Greenock to Martinique in May 1762. [NAS.E504.15.11]

GLASGOW, master John Dunn, arrived in Boston, New England, in January 1770 from Greenock. [BoNL#3459]

GLASGOW, master Soloman Townsend, from Fort William *with 260 passengers* bound for New York in September 1775, arrived there but redirected to Boston, landed there on 8 December 1775. [NA.AO2.495/551]

GLASGOW, Captain Taylor, from Glasgow on 30 May 1824 *with 7 passengers* bound for Quebec, arrived there on 4 August 1824. [CC.11.8.1824]

GLEN OF NEW YORK, master John Rodgers, from Inverkeithing to New York in October 1810. [NAS.E504.16.1]

GLENCAIRN OF GLASGOW, master James Glasgow, from Port Glasgow to Jamaica in November 1747; from Port Glasgow to Jamaica in October 1748. [NAS.E504.28.3/4]

GLENIFFER, Captain Stevenson, arrived in Quebec during July 1826 *with 42 passengers* from Greenock. [QM: 29.7.1826]

GLENTANNAR, Captain Murray, from Tobermory *with 147 passengers* on 8 July 1820, of whom 129 were landed on Cape Breton, and 18 in Quebec on 25 August 1820, [QM]; master William Walker, from Aberdeen to Quebec in July 1826, [NAS.E504.1.32]

GLORY, master James Grant, arrived in Quebec on 28 August 1819 from Aberdeen. [MG:8.9.1819]

GOOD INTENT, Captain Thompson, from Aberdeen on 8 May 1824 *with 1 passenger* bound for Quebec, arrived there on 23 June 1824. [CC.30.6.1824]

GORDOMAN PHOENIX, master John Gordon, bound from Scotland to Charles Island, Nova Scotia, in 1627. [NAS.AC7.1.184]

GORDON GALLEY, master Charles Gordon, was captured by the Spanish off the coast of New Spain in 1714. [ACA.APB.2.123]

GOWAN, a brig, master James Webster, arrived in Quebec on 12 May 1818 from Dundee. [MG]

GRACE OF KIRKCUDBRIGHT, (Gordon of Lochinvar's ship), to America after 8 October 1626. [DBR, Kenmure Charter chest]

GRACE AND MOLLY OF BELFAST, master Thomas Lyle, from Port Glasgow via Belfast to Barbados in January 1748. [NAS.E504.28.3]

GRANDVALE, master William Hamilton, from Port Glasgow bound for Jamaica via Grenada and St Kitts in January 1771, *'tradesmen will meet with proper encouragement'*. [CM#7594]

GRATITUDE, a 175 ton brig, Captain Gellatly, from Fort William on 26 July 1824 *with 38 passengers* bound for Quebec, arrived there on 13 September 1824; from Dundee on 27 March 1825 *with passengers* bound for Quebec, arrive dthere on 25 May 1825; from Dundee on 24 August 1825 bound for

Quebec, arrived on 21 October 1825; from Leith *with* passengers bound for Quebec on 12 April 1826, arrived there on 30 May 1836; from Dundee to Quebec and Montreal in January 1829. [CC.18.9.1824][CCMA: 1.6.1825; 26.10.1825; 7.6.1826] [NAS.E504.11.26]

GREENFIELDS, a brig, Captain Holmes, arrived in Quebec on 20 May 1818 *with 3 passengers* from Glasgow. [MG]

GREENOCK OF GREENOCK, a brig, master John Orr arrived in the York River, Virginia, on 2 June 1738 *with 6 passengers* from Greenock; sailed for Greenock on 21 August 1738; master James Crawford, from Virginia on 2 June 1740, arrived in Greenock on 19 July 1740; master John Gray, from Greenock to Virginia on 21 March 1741; arrived in Greenock on 21 November 1741 from Virginia; master Thomas Young, from Greenock to St Kitts in July 1743. [VaGaz#98/108][CM#3171/3276/3309][NAS.E504.15.1]

GREENOCK OF GREENOCK, master James Butcher, arrived in Upper District, James River, Virginia, on 23 July 1737 via Boston; master Thomas Malcolm, from Greenock to Jamaica in January 1768. [VaGaz.5.8.1737][NAS.E504.15.15]

GREENOCK OF INVERKEITHING, master John Roxburgh, arrived in Aberdeen from Maryland in March 1749. [NAS.E504.1.3]

GRIZZY OF AYR, master Hugh Boyd, from Ayr to Antigua, April 1758; master William McLean, from Stranraer, Wigtownshire, to Antigua on 8 January 1759. [NAS.E504.4.3; E504.34.2]

HAMILTON OF GLASGOW, later OF RENFREW, master John Scott, from Greenock to Virginia on 12 May 1741. [CN#3299]; from Port Glasgow to Jamaica in February 1744. [NAS.E504.28.1]

HAMLET, Captain Christie, from Greenock on 4 April 1824, arrived in Quebec on 19 May 1824. [MG:26.5.1824]

HANNA MARIA OF WHITEHAVEN, master Henry Wood, arrived on 21 October 1723 at Carsethorn, Dumfries, from Virginia. [Dumfries Customs Records]

HANNAH OF GREENOCK, a snow, master Stephen Rowand, from Greenock to Jamaica in November 1763; master James Crawford, arrived in Savannah, Georgia, on 11 October 1767 from Jamaica. [NAS.E504.15.12][NA.CO5/709]

HANNAH, a 138 ton brig, Captain Martin, from Dundee on 17 July 1823 bound for New York, arrived there on 15 September 1823. [DPCA#1089/1096/1102]

HANNAH MOORE, Captain Black, arrived in Quebec on 30 May 1820 *with 3 passengers* from Aberdeen. [QM]

HANNIBAL, from Dundee to Jamaica in December 1828 and in December 1829. [NAS.E504.11.26]

HANOVER OF BELFAST, a brigantine, master James Weir, from Port Glasgow to Barbados in September 1716, [NAS.E508.10.6]

HANOVER OF IRVINE, master John Boyd, from Irvine, Ayrshire, to Virginia, 1728. [NAS.AC10.136]

HANOVER, master Robert Pollock, from Port Glasgow to Jamaica in February 1777, [NAS.E504.28.27]

HARDICANUTE or HARDIKNUT, master Robert Rogers, from the Clyde to Virginia in 1735, arrived in Port Glasgow on 30 December 1735 from Virginia; master John Lyon, arrived in the James River, Virginia, in May 1737 from Glasgow, returned to Glasgow on 16 July 1737. [GHG#210][NAS.E512/1455][VG:6.5.1737][VaGaz#40]

HARMONY, master Thomas Alexander, from Greenock to Port Antonio, Port Maria, and Oraccabessa, Jamaica, in March 1802. [GA#2]

HARMONY, a brig, arrived in Quebec on 22 August 1819 *with 253 passengers* from Oban, Argyllshire; Captain Nichol, arrived in Quebec on 31 May 1821 *with 2 passengers* from Leith;

Captain Spence, from Greenock on 30 April 1822, arrived in Quebec on 12 June 1822; from Leith on 16 July 1825 *with passengers* bound for Quebec, arrived there on 25 August 1825; Captain Young, arrived in Quebec during May 1828 *with 79 passengers* from Leith; from Ayr to Chaleur Bay, New Brunswick, in April 1827 and in April 1828; from Ayr to Dalhousie, New Brunswick, in July 1828 and in April 1829. [MG: 1.9.1819; 6.6.1821; 19.6.1822] [CCMA:31.8.1825][QM: 24.8.1819/20.5.1828] [NAS.E504.4.15]

HARMONY, a 154 ton snow, master J. Morgan, from Greenock to Pictou in 1821. [L]

HARMONY, from Leith to Quebec in April 1829. [NAS.E504.22.127]

HARRIOT, 200 tons, master Thomas Herdman, arrived in Virginia in July 1767 from Aberdeen; from Aberdeen *with passengers* to Maderia, Barbados, Grenada, Antigua and Virginia in February 1768. [VG:6.7.1767][AJ#1041/1044]

HAWK OF GLASGOW, master Colin Campbell, from Greenock to Jamaica in April 1763; James Clark, from Greenock to Antigua in January 1767, and from Greenock to Jamaica in November 1767. [NAS.E504.15.11/14/15]

HEART OF OAK, Captain Booth, from Aberdeen on 2 April 1825 *with passengers* bound for Quebec, arrived there on 13 May 1825; from Aberdeen on 26 July 1825 bound for Quebec, arrived there on 13 September 1825; from Aberdeen on 4 April 1826 bound for Quebec, arrived there on 16 May 1826. [CCMA: 18.5.1825; 17.9.1825; 20.5.1826]

HECTOR, a brig, master James Webster, arrived in Quebec on 30 May 1835 *with 3 passengers* from Dundee. [MG:9.6.1819]

HECTOR, from Greenock *with passengers* bound for New York, arrived there on 17 August 1825, [NARA.M237.7]; from Dundee to New York in October 1828. [NAS.E504.11.26]

HELEN, master James Seaman, from Leith to Charleston, 1734. [NAS.AC9.1960]

HELEN, master Robert Workman, from Greenock via Cork to Grenada in November 1763; from Greenock to Montserrat in December 1764. [NAS.E504.15.12]

HELEN OF DUNDEE, master Thomas Erskine, from Dundee on 19 April 1821 *with 35 passengers* bound for Quebec, arrived there on 12 June 1821; arrived in Quebec on 22 May 1823 *with 20 passengers* from Dundee on 11 April 1823. [MG:20.6.1821][QM:23.5.1823][CC:28.5.1823]

HELEN AND MARY OF MONTROSE, master Joseph Macintosh, from Anstruther, Fife, to Barbados in September 1717. [NAS.E508.11.6]

HELEN DOUGLAS, from Dumfries to New Brunswick in April 1826. [DWJ.11.4.1826]

HENDRY AND ANN OF MARYLAND, master Samuel Wilson, arrived in Port Glasgow on 7 July 1690 from Virginia. [NAS.E72.15.18]

HENRY OF GLASGOW, master John Clarke, from Port Glasgow to Barbados in January 1716 and in December 1716, [NAS.E508.10.6/11.6]

HENRY, Captain Thompson, from Greenock on 4 August 1823, arrived in Quebec on 26 September 1823. [CC:26.9.1823]

HERALD, Captain Moore, from Greenock on 21 August 1817 *with 2 passengers* bound for Quebec, arrived there in October 1817. [MG: 15.10.1817]

HERALD, from Dundee to Charleston in August 1829. [NAS.E504.11.26]

HERBERTS, Captain Campbell, from Greenock to Grenada on 16 March 1802. [GA#20]

HERCULES, master Edward Say, from Leith to Virginia in September 1673. [NAS.E72.15.17]

HERCULES OF MONTROSE, master Alexander Gordon, from Inverness to Barbados in September 1715, [NAS.E508.10.6]

HERCULES OF AYR, master John McGowan, from Ayr to St John's, Newfoundland, in June 1764; from Ayr to St John's in April 1766; from Ayr to Antigua in June 1770. [NAS.E504.4.3/4/5]

HERCULES, master Moses Cadenhead, from Aberdeen to Grenada, Dominica, Tobago, Barbados, and Jamaica in January 1775; master James Davidson, from Aberdeen to New York on 6 June 1777. [AJ#1400/1529/1535]

HERCULES, Captain Crawford, from the Clyde to Jamaica in August 1802. [GA#1/64]

HERCULES, Captain Kay, arrived in Quebec on 8 September 1822 *with 4 passengers* from Greenock. [MG:14.9.1822]

HERCULES, from Dundee to Savannah, Georgia, in August 1829. [NAS.E504.11.26]

HERO OF AYR, master John Bowie, from Ayr to Antigua and Montserrat in February 1769, and in March 1770; master John Johnston, from Ayr to Antigua in October 1773. [NAS.E504.4.5/6]

HERO, Captain Fleck, from Port Glasgow to St Kitts in May 1802. [GA#1/34]

HERO, master Robert Wilson, from Greenock to Quebec in July 1802. [GA#1/62]

HERO, from Dundee to New York in October 1829. [NAS.E504.11.26]

HIGHLAND LAD, Captain Moore, arrived in Quebec on 12 May 1818 from Greenock; Captain Vickerman, arrived in Quebec during September 1826 *with 16 passengers* from Tobermory, Mull, Argyll. [MG][QM: 23.9.1826]

HIGHLANDER, Captain Birnie, from Aberdeen to Quebec in August 1826, [NAS.E504.1.32]

H.M.S. HERALD, Commander Leeke, from Greenock on 11 August 1825 *with passengers* bound for Quebec, arrived there on 16 September 1825. [CCMA:21.9.1825]

HOMER, master Robert Hastie, arrived in the James River, Virginia, on 29 August 1768 from Glasgow via the Isle of May. [VG:1.9.1768]

HOPE OF PORT GLASGOW, 70 tons, arrived in the Clyde from Virginia in 1711. [SC: 26.2.1711]

HOPE, a brigantine, master George Urquhart, from Leith via Cromarty to South Carolina, 1736. [NAS.AC7.44.287; AC8.599; AC9.1605; AC10.227]

HOPE, master John Smith, from Ayr to Philadelphia in January 1760. [NAS.E504.4.3]

HOPE, master M. Henry, arrived in Quebec during October 1806 *with passengers* from Port Glasgow. [QM: 30.10.1806]

HOPE, Captain Trotter, arrived in Quebec on 4 August 1817 from Grangemouth. [MG]

HOPE, master John Duncan, arrived in Quebec in September 1819 from Greenock. [MG.27.9.1819]

HOPE, master Ninian Warden, arrived in Quebec *with 164 passengers* from Oban. [MG:1.9.1819]

HOPE, master J. Duncan, arrived in Quebec on 14 August 1820 *with 44 passengers* from Greenock. [QM]

HOPE, Captain Ganson, from Aberdeen to Miramichi, New Brunswick, in April 1826, [NAS.E504.1.32]

HOPKIRK, master Neil Campbell, from Greenock to Jamaica in April 1763; master Colin Campbell, from Greenock to Jamaica in March 1766; master John Sprott, arrived in Savannah, Georgia, on 8 November 1766 from Jamaica; master Colin Campbell, from Greenock to Jamaica in October 1767; [NAS.E504.15.11/13/15][NA.CO5/709]

HORTOUN OF GLASGOW, master Robert Arthur, from
Greenock to Antigua in October 1714. [NAS.E508.8.6]

HOULIKAN OF BELFAST, master John Jackson, from Stranraer,
Wigtownshire, to Barbados on 30 April 1746; master William
King, from Port Glasgow to Jamaica in December 1748.
[NAS.E504.28.4; E504.34.1]

HOUSTON, master James Orr, from Greenock to Martinique and St
Kitts in September 1762; master Robert Chisholm, from
Greenock to St Kitts in February 1765; master John Simpson,
from Greenock to St Kitts in January 1766.
[NAS.E504.15.11/12/13/14]

HOWARD, an American ship, master George Fram, from Greenock
to New York on 23 August 1802. [GA#1/48, 67]

HUME, master Duncan McLean, from Port Glasgow to Jamaica in
September 1776, [NAS.E504.28.26]
HUNTER OF IRVINE, master John Robinson, from Ayr to
Dominica in February 1776. [NAS.E504.4.6]

HUNTER, Captain Rodger, from Greenock to New Providence on
20 April 1802. [GA#1/33]

HUNTLEY, Captain Wilson, arrived in Quebec during August 1829
with 176 passengers from Greenock. [QM:15.8.1829]

IDA, from Inverkeithing to Jamaica in November 1827.
[NAS.E504.16.1]

INDEPENDENT, Captain McLarty, from Greenock to
Newfoundland on 3 April 1802; Captain Walker, from the
Clyde to Newfoundland 9 September 1802. [GA#1/26, 72]

INDIAN, Captain Turnbull, from Grangemouth on 7 April 1824,
arrived in Quebec on 2 June 1824; Captain Matthias, arrived
in Quebec during September 1827 *with 69 passengers* from
Greenock. [MG:9.6.1824][QM: 7.9.1827]

INDUSTRY OF GLASGOW, master William Houston, from the
Clyde to St Kitts in 1735. [GHG#210]; master Robert Kelso,

from Port Glasgow to St Kitts in October 1739; master Robert
Kelso, from Greenock to St Kitts on 30 July 1740; master
Adam Chisholm, from Greenock to St Kitts on 30 April 1741.
[CM#3032/3176/3292]

INDUSTRY OF ABERDEEN, 70 tons, master John Ross, from
Aberdeen to Antigua in March 1752. [NAS.E504.1.4]

INDUSTRY OF LEITH, 100 tons, master Andrew Cowan, from
Leith to South Carolina in September 1754. [NAS.E504.22.6]

INDUSTRY OF LEITH, 85 tons. master James MacLuckie, from
Inverkeithing to Quebec in April 1812. [NAS.E504.16.1]

INGRAM, master William Hunter, from Greenock to Grenada in
September 1763. [NAS.E504.15.11]

INTEGRITY, a 163 ton brig, Captain Emmerson, from Greenock to
Pictou, Nova Scotia, and Miramichi, New Brunswick, in
August 1816. [GC:8.1816]

INVINCIBLE, master J. Hogg, arrived in Quebec on 15 May 1818
from Peterhead. [MG]

ISABEL OF BELFAST, master Richard Garnet, arrived in Port
Glasgow on 7 October 1682 from Barbados. [NAS.E72.19.5]

ISABELLA OF GREENOCK, master Abraham Hastie, arrived in
the Potomac River twice between 1710 and 1718 via
Barbados. [VSS#35/37]

ISABELLA, master Frederick Symons, from Leith to New York in
October 1753. [NAS.E504.22.5]

ISABELLA, master Angus McLarty, from Greenock to St Kitts and
Grenada in October 1764; master William Hodgyard, from
Greenock to Grenada in October 1765. [NAS.E504.15.12/13]

ISABELLA, Captain King, from Greenock to St Kitts on 17
February 1802. [GA#9]

ISABELLA, Captain Paterson, from the Clyde to Tortola on 30
June 1802. [GA#1/51]

ISABELLA, 313 tons, master W. Sharp, from Greenock to Quebec in 1808. [L]

ISABELLA, a brig, master D. Pratt, arrived in Quebec on 17 June 1818 from Aberdeen. [MG:24.6.1818]

ISABELLA OF WIGTOWN, from Wigtown to Richibucto, New Brunswick, in August 1828. [NAS.E504.37.7]

JAMAICA PACKET OF BURNTISLAND, master Thomas Smith, from Kirkcaldy, Fife, to Antigua in October 1774, [NAS.E504.20.8]

JAMES OF GLASGOW, master William Anderson, from Glasgow to Virginia on 28 December 1685, [NAS.E72.19.12]; master John Mearns, arrived in Port Glasgow on 1 September 1696 from St Kitts. [NAS.E72.15.23]

JAMES, master James Melville, from Virginia to Dunbar, 1727. [NAS.AC9.1016]

JAMES OF GREENOCK, master James Scott, from Greenock to Barbados in October 1728. [NAS.E508.22.6/32, 51]

JAMES OF DUNDEE, 150 tons, Captain John Traill, from Leith *with passengers* to Boston, New England, on 10 June 1739; master John Traill, arrived in Leith on 31 August 1740 from New England; from Leith *with passengers* in September (?) 1740; arrived in Leith on 22 August 1741 from Boston; from Leith to Boston *with passengers* in March 1742. [CM#2993/3182/3187/3335/3341]; from Leith to Virginia in 1748. [NAS.AC10.339]

JAMES OF PORT GLASGOW, master James Orr, from Greenock to Virginia on 31 January 1741. [CM#3255]

JAMES OF LEITH, 140 tons, master William Watson, from Leith to Grenada in October 1773. [NAS.E504.22.18]

JAMES, Captain Jack, arrived in Quebec on 8 August 1817 *with 24 passengers* from Greenock. [MG]

JAMES, Captain Henderson, arrived in Quebec on 29 July 1819 from Aberdeen. [MG:4.8.1819]

JAMES AND MARGARET OF DUNDEE, master James Patrick, from Dundee to Antigua in February 1764. [NAS.E504.11.5] **JAMES AND MARGARET,** Captain Milne, from Aberdeen to New York in May 1826, [NAS.E504.1.32]

JAMES MONTGOMERY, master W. Holmes, arrived in Quebec on 14 September 1817 *with 11 passengers* from Greenock; Captain Gardner, arrived in Quebec on 19 May 1818 from Glasgow. [MG]

JAN, Captain Thom, arrived in Quebec on 7 May 1819 from Montrose. [MG:19.5.1819]

JANE OF GLASGOW, a snow, master William Butcher, arrived in the York River, Virginia, on 25 June 1745 from Glasgow. [VaGaz#466]

JANE, master Thomas Glen, from Ayr to Antigua in April 1750. [NAS.E504.4.2]

JANE, a brig, arrived in Kingston, Jamaica, in July 1794 *with 7 passengers* from Greenock; Captain Miller, from Greenock to Grenada on 3 April 1802. [Royal Gazette:2.8.1794] [GA#1/26]

JANE, a brig, master Alexander Murdoch, arrived in Quebec on 21 October 1817 from Ayr; arrived in Quebec on 19 May 1818 *with 18 passengers* from Greenock; from Irvine on 1 August 1818, arrived in Quebec on 9 September 1818; from Greenock on 12 April 1819, arrived in Quebec on 21 May 1819; from Greenock on 22 August 1819 *with 13 passengers* bound for Quebec, arrived there in October 1819; from Greenock on 6 April 1820, arrived in Quebec on 2 June 1820; arrived in Quebec on 11 October 1820 *with 5 passengers* from Ayr. [MG: 5.11.1817; 2.6.1819; 20.10.1819]

JANE, Captain Roger, arrived in Quebec on 7 September 1819 *with 64 passengers* from Greenock; arrived in Quebec on 23 August 1818 *with 131 passengers* from Greenock. [MG: 15.9.1819]

JANE, master W. Allan, arrived in Quebec on 19 May 1820 *with 34 passengers* from Greenock; from Greenock on 9 April 1823 *with 11 passengers* bound for Quebec, arrived there on 20 May 1823; from Greenock on 22 August 1823 *with 2 passengers* bound for Quebec, arrived there on 2 October 1823. [QM: 19.5.1820][CC:24.5.1823; 8.10.1823]

JANE, Captain Snowden, from Greenock on 13 June 1823 *with 69 passengers* bound for Quebec, arrived there on 26 July 1823; Captain Wright, from Greenock on 7 June 1824 *with 50 passengers* bound for Quebec, arrived there on 3 August 1824. [CC:2.8.1823; 7.8.1824]

JANE OF CAMPBELTOWN, master James Murchy, from Campbeltown, Argyll, to New Richmond, Quebec, on 5 April 1824. [NAS.E504.8.10]

JANE, from Greenock to New Orleans in October 1829. [NAS.E504.15.170]

JANE HADDOW, a 345 ton brig, master James Hamilton, from Greenock to New York in January 1831. [GA#3610]

JANE HASTIE, from Greenock *with passengers* bound for New York, arrived there on 27 July 1829. [NARA.M237/13]

JANE HATTON, from Greenock to Newfoundland in October 1829. [NAS.E504.15.170]

JANE WRIGHT, arrived in Quebec during August 1824 *with 50 passengers* from Greenock. [QM:3.8.1824]

JANET, master George Boag, from Glasgow to the Canary Islands in 1705. [CalSPDom.SP44/392/75]

JANET OF GREENOCK, master William Petteerue, from Greenock to Barbados in January 1717, [NAS.E508.10.6]

JANET OF GLASGOW, master Samuel Bowman, arrived in Greenock on 27 December 1740 from Virginia. [CM#3240]

JANET, a brig, Captain Oliphant, from Greenock on 8 May 1825, arrived in Quebec on 21 June 1825. [CCMA: 29.6.1825]

JANET AND ANNE, 140 tons, master George Craik, from Aberdeen to Madeira, Grenada, Antigua and Jamaica *with passengers* in February 1769, also in February 1770, and from Aberdeen to Grenada and Jamaica in December 1772; master John Yule, from Aberdeen to Grenada and Jamaica in 1773 also in January 1775. [AJ#1096/1143/1280/1307/1399]

JANET DUNLOP, a brig, master D. Lamont, from Greenock to Honduras in 1831. [GA#3610]

JASON, Captain Gourlie, from the Clyde to Antigua in August 1802. [GA#1/64]

JEAN OF LEITH, from Leith to Greenland in 1686. [RPCS.XII.482]

JEAN OF CRAWFORDDYKES, [formerly the **BRISBANE**] 120 tons, from Virginia to Glasgow by 1723. [NAS.AC9.818]

JEAN OF GREENOCK, master John Easdale, from Greenock to Jamaica, 1730. [NAS.AC9.1104]

JEAN OF GLASGOW, master Patrick Jack, from the Clyde to Virginia in 1735. [GHG#210]; arrived at the Sound of Mull, Argyll, on 26 February 1741 and on 28 February in Greenock, from Virginia; master Patrick Jack, from Greenock to Virginia on 12 May 1741; arrived in Greenock on 16 January 1742 from Virginia; from Greenock to Virginia on 1 May 1742; arrived in Port Glasgow on 1 November 1742 from Virginia. [CM#3265/3267/3299/3333/3378][NAS.E504.28.1]

JEAN, master John Smith, from Ely, Fife, in December 1770 bound for St Kitts, *'a blacksmith and a cooper are wanted to go out by this ship'.* [CM#7596]

JEAN, master John Ritchie, from Port Glasgow to Antigua in May 1776. [NAS.E504.28.26]

JEAN, 192 tons, master William Anderson, from Greenock to New York, later bound for Jamaica and Antigua, in August 1802. [GA#1/60, 67]

JEAN OF IRVINE, Captain Wilson, arrived in Quebec during May 1805 *with passengers* from Greenock. [QM: 18.5.1805]

JEAN, master Thomas Innes, arrived in Quebec on 10 September 1819 from Aberdeen. [MG.22.9.1819]

JEAN, a brig, master Alexander Allan, arrived in Quebec on 2 August 1819 *with 28 passengers* from Greenock; arrived in Quebec on 26 May 1821 from Greenock; from Greenock on 3 April 1822 *with 30 passengers* bound for Quebec, arrived there on 15 May 1822; from Greenock on 6 April 1824 *with 16 passengers* bound for Quebec, arrived there on 3 June 1824; from Greenock on 26 August 1824 *with 5 passengers* bound for Quebec, arrived there on 3 October 1824; Captain Currie, from Greenock *with passengers,* on 7 April 1825, arrived there on 14 May 1825. [MG: 11.8.1819; 6.6.1821; 29.5.1822; 9.6.1824] [CC.13.10.1824] [CCMA: 21.5.25]

JEAN, Captain Masterton, from Leith on 10 April 1824, arrived in Quebec on 6 June 1824. [MG.9.6.1824]

JEAN AND BETTY, master Patrick Gordon, from Greenock to St Kitts in January 1763; from Greenock to St Kitts in October 1764. [NAS.E504.15.11/12]

JEAN AND ELIZABETH OF HARTLEPOOL, master William Baxter, arrived in Aberdeen on 4 June 1750 from Virginia. [NAS.E504.1.3]

JEAN AND ELIZABETH OF ABERDEEN, 100 tons, master Thomas Smith, from Aberdeen to Virginia in September 1751. [NAS.E504.1.4]

JEAN AND WILLIAM OF GLASGOW, to New England in 1678. [NAS.AC7.4]

JEAN HASTIE, from Greenock to Halifax, Nova Scotia, in October 1829. [NAS.E504.15.170]

JEANIE, master John Cowan, from Greenock to City Point, James River, Virginia, in July 1802. [GA#1/45]

JEANNIE OF GLASGOW, master James Lyon, from Greenock to St Kitts in January 1767 and in January 1768. [NAS.E504.15.14/15]

JEANNIE OF CAMPBELTOWN, master Alexander McLarty, from Greenock to Antigua in February 1768. [NAS.E504.15.15]

JEANNIE, master David Cumming, from Port Glasgow to Tobago in November 1776; from Port Glasgow to Tobago in October 1777. [NAS.E504.28.26/27]

JEANY, master Hugh Maxwell, from Greenock to St Kitts in September 1762; master James Lyon, from Greenock to St Kitts in September 1765; master John Wood, from Greenock to St Kitts in August 1767. [NAS.E504.15.11/13/14]

JENNY OF GLASGOW, master Samuel Bowman, from Greenock to Virginia on 30 April 1741; arrived in Greenock on 16 January 1742 from Virginia; from Greenock to Virginia on 23 March 1742; Captain Bogle, from Glasgow on 18 March 1745, arrived in the James River, Virginia, in May 1745. [CM#3292/3333/3361][VG#460]

JENNY, arrived in Dumfries on 24 November 1760 from Virginia. [Dumfries Customs Records]

JENNY OF IRVINE, a brig, master Robert Caldwell, arrived in Savannah, Georgia, on 21 January 1766 from St Christophers; from Ayr to New York in September 1767. [NA.CO5/709][NAS.E504.4.4]

JENNY, master Thomas Archdeacon, from Greenock to St Kitts in October 1763; master Robert Ewing, from Greenock to Antigua in August 1766 and in August 1767. [NAS.E504.15.12/13/14]

JENNY, master John Reid, from Port Glasgow to Halifax, Nova Scotia, in December 1776, [E504.28.26]

JESSIE, brigantine, master Thomas Boag, from Greenock to
Quebec in March 1802, also sailed 23 August 1802.
[GA#1/15, 67]

JESSIE, a brig, from Annan, Dumfries-shire, to Miramichi, New
Brunswick, in July 1817; from Glencaple, Dumfries-shire, to
Philadelphia in 1818; from Glencaple to America in 1822;
from Glencaple to New Brunswick in 1828. [DWJ.29.7.1817;
7.4.1818; 13.8.1822; 11.3.1828]

JESSIE, master James Thompson, arrived in Quebec on 30 July
1817 *with 14 passengers* from Aberdeen. [MG]

JESSIE, a 219 ton brig, master W. Lyon, FROM Greenock to
Savannah in 1819; arrived in Quebec on 1 October 1819 from
Ayr; from Greenock to Miramachi in 1820.
[MG.13.10.1819][L]

JESSIE, Captain Hardy, arrived in Quebec on 10 October 1823
from Greenock. [CC:18.10.1823]

JESSIE LAWSON, Captain Hall, from Greenock on 7 August 1825
bound for Quebec, arrived there on 17 September 1825.
[CCMA:21.9.1825]

JESSIES, from Leith to Montreal in April 1829. [NAS.E04.22.127]

JOANNA OF ABERDEEN, 130 tons, master Alexander Inglis,
from Virginia in August 1710 via Careston, Orkney, to
Aberdeen, arrived there on 18 January 1711,
[ACA.APB.31.1.1711]; to Virginia in 1711, captured by a
French privateer but later ransomed. [SC: 26.5.1711]
[ECA.Moses#141/5495]

JOANNA OF GLASGOW, master Walter Nimmo, from Greenock
to St Kitts in January 1768. [NAS.E504.15.15]

JOHANNA, a brig, from Dumfries to Antigua in 1788.
[DWJ.22.1.1788]

JOHN OF LONDON, master James Moodie, arrived in Glasgow
on 27 October 1686 from the West Indies. [NAS.E72.19.12]

JOHN OF LONDONDERRY, master Andrew Cruikshank, arrived in Port Glasgow on 17 September 1691 from Virginia. [NAS.E72.15.21]

JOHN OF PORTSMOUTH, NEW HAMPSHIRE, a brigantine, from Boston to Leith by 1739. [NAS.AC7.44.185, 268]

JOHN OF PORT GLASGOW, master John McCall, from Port Glasgow to Jamaica in December 1745. [NAS.E504.28.2]

JOHN OF IRVINE, master John Francis, from Port Glasgow to New York in October 1747. [NAS.E504.28.3]

JOHN OF KIRKCUDBRIGHT, master John Paul (Jones), to the West Indies, 1770. [NAS.SC16.12.14; RH1.2.697]

JOHN, Captain Mitchell, arrived in Quebec on 19 August 1817 *with 118 passengers* from Leith; master Peter Todd, from Inverkeithing to Montreal *with 1 passenger* on 29 April 1823, arrived in Quebec on 19 June 1823; from Inverkeithing to Montreal *with passengers* on 10 April 1824, arrived in Quebec on 4 June 1824; from Inverkeithing to Quebec in July 1827. [MG: 9.6.1824] [NAS.E504.16.1][CC:25.6.1823]

JOHN, a brig, from Greenock on 8 June 1825 bound for Quebec, arrived there on 14 August 1825. [CCMA: 20.8.1825]

JOHN AND DAVID OF PORT GLASGOW, a snow, to Barbados in 1728. [NAS.AC10.138]

JOHN AND MARGARET, master John Masson, from Aberdeen on 11 April 1819, arrived in Quebec on 19 May 1819. [MG: 26.5.1819]

JOHN AND MARJORY OF MONTROSE, master John Sangster, from Montrose, Angus, to Jamaica in January 1747. [NAS.E504.24.1]

JOHN AND MATTY OF BELFAST, master John Russell, from Campbeltown, Argyll, to Antigua in January 1776. [NAS.E504.8.5]

JOHN AND ROBERT OF GOUROCK, master Thomas Clark, from Greenock to Barbados in September 1727, [NAS.E508.22.6/48]; from the Clyde to St Kitts in 1735. [GHG#210]; master James Orr, from Greenock on 14 March 1741 to Virginia; arrived in Greenock on 19 September 1741 from Virginia; from Greenock to Virginia on 20 February 1742; from Greenock via the Isle of May to Barbados in September 1743. [CM#3273/3355/3350][NAS.E504.15.1]

JOHN DICKENSON, from Greenock *with passengers* bound for New York, arrived there on 12 August 1824. [NARA.M237.6]

JOSEPH AND DANIEL, master David Ferguson, from Ayr via Madeira to Virginia or Maryland in 1693, captured by Ostend privateers on return voyage in 1694. [AA.B6.35.6]

JOSEPH HUME, from Greenock *with passengers* bound for New York, arrived there on 26 October 1829. [NARA.M237.13]

JUDITH, master Joseph Hunter, from Ayr via Dublin to Barbados in January 1755; from Ayr to Barbados in October 1756. [NAS.E504.4.2/3]

JULIAN, Captain Smith, from Greenock on 17 August 1822, arrived in Quebec on 7 October 1822. [MG:12.10.1822]

JULIANA, a brig, Captain Scott, from Dundee to New York in November 1823. [DPCA#1110]

JUNO, from Greenock to Quebec in July 1802, sailed 23 August 1802. [GA#1/58, 67]

JUNO, a brig, Captain Henderson, arrived in Quebec on 16 June 1817 *with 20 passengers* from Dundee; arrived in Quebec on 7 June 1818 from Dundee; arrived in Quebec on 15 May 1821 *with 6 passengers* from Aberdeen. [MG:23.6.1817; 17.6.1818; 23.5.1821]

JUPITER OF ABERDEEN, a snow, master Arthur Gibbon, from Aberdeen *with passengers* to Kingston, Jamaica, on 30 April 1761. [AJ#681/690]

KATHERINE OF LONDON, master John Lakey, from Glasgow to Virginia on 29 December 1685. [NAS.E72.19.12]

KATHERINE OF GLASGOW, master James Wilson, arrived in Glasgow on 10 September 1686 from Virginia; master Andrew Crookshanks, from Port Glasgow to Madeira in October 1691. [NAS.E72.19.12/22]

KATHERINE OF BARBADOS, master James Hays, arrived in Stranraer, Scotland, in May 1757 from Charleston, then sailed to Belfast. [NAS.E504.34.3]

KATY, master William Harvie, from Port Glasgow to New York in May 1777. [NAS.E504.28.27]

KENNERSLEY CASTLE, master Henry Crouch, from Leith *with 171 passengers* to Poyais in January 1823. [LCL.X.1025] {arrived there on 20 March 1823}

KENT, Captain Stirling, arrived in Quebec on 26 June 1821 *with 50 passengers* from Greenock; from Ayr to the Bay of Chaleur, New Brunswick, in September 1825. [MG:27.6.1821] [NAS.E504.4.15]

KINGSTON OF GLASGOW, master Adam Chisholm, from Port Glasgow via Cork to St Kitts in October 1742; from Port Glasgow via Cork to St Kitts in October 1743; from Port Glasgow to Jamaica in October 1744; from Port Glasgow to Jamaica in October 1745. [NAS.E504.28.1/2]; John Campbell, from Greenock to Jamaica in March 1765. [NAS.E504.15.12]

KINGSTON, master James Ryburn, from Ayr to North Carolina on 23 November 1757; from Ayr to Barbados in November 1758. [NAS.E504.4.3]

KINNOULL OF LEITH, 100 tons, master Alexander Alexander, from Leith to St Kitts in September 1765. [NAS.E504.22.12]

KIRKCONNELL OF DUMFRIES, from Dumfries *with passengers* to Virginia in December 1714. [DGA:GF4.19A/10]

LADY NEILSON, Captain Beck, from Greenock to New Providence on 10 February 1802. [GA#9]

LARCH, a brig, Captain Beatson, from Aberdeen *with passengers* on 1 May 1826, arrived in Quebec on 12 June 1826. [CCMA:17.6.1826]

LARK OF LONDON, master George Rodgers, from Inverness to Jamaica in November 1728. [NAS.E508.22.6/76,77]

LARK, Captain Wells, arrived in Quebec on 14 June 1817 from Peterhead. [MG:23.6.1817]

LATONA, Captain Morris, from Aberdeen on 29 April 1823, arrived in Quebec on 9 June 1823. [CC:14.6.1823]

LAUDON, master James King, from Greenock to Antigua in November 1758. [NAS.E504.15.9]

LAUREL OF ABERDEEN, master John Coutts, from Aberdeen to Jamaica in April 1752. [NAS.E504.1.4]

LAUREL OF GREENOCK, master James Lang, from Greenock to Jamaica in November 1758. [NAS.E504.15.9]

LAVINIA, master Alexander Keith, arrived in Quebec on 9 September 1819 *with 21 passengers from the wrecked Lovely Nelly.* [MG:15.9.1819]

LEAH, a brig, master William Andrew, arrived in Hampton, Virginia, on 9 March 1745 from Glasgow. [VG#457]

LEAH OF LONDON, master David Fraser, arrived in Montrose on 22 June 1748 from the James River, Virginia. [NAS.CE53.1.4]

LEANDER, Captain Stewart, from the Clyde on 10 April 1802 bound for New Providence. [GA#1/28]

LEATHLY OF ABERDEEN, master John Lickly, from Aberdeen to Virginia on 15 June 1748. [NAS.E504.1.2]

LEITH GALLEY OF LEITH, 200 tons, master John Sharp, from Leith to Kingston, Jamaica, in January 1753, also in October 1754. [NAS.E504.22.5/6]

LEONIDAS, from Greenock *with passengers* to New Orleans, arrived there on 19 January 1826. [NARA:M259/5]

LEOPARD OF IRVINE, master Colin Finlay, from Port Glasgow to Barbados in November 1713, [NAS.E508.7.6]

LETITIA OF VIRGINIA, master John Wall, arrived in Aberdeen in May 1751 from Aberdeen, then sailed to Barbados in June 1751. [NAS.E504.1.4]

LIBERTY, master William Smith, from the Clyde to Boston in 1735, arrived in Port Glasgow on 5 January 1736 from Boston. [GHG#210][NAS.E512/1455]

LIBERTY OF GLASGOW, master Andrew Syme, arrived in Greenock on 28 March 1741 from Virginia. [CM#3279]

LIBERTY, master Hugh Smellie, from Port Glasgow to St Kitts in February 1770. [CM#7419]

LIDDLE, a brig, Captain Thompson, from Leith on 29 July 1825 bound for Quebec, arrived there on 16 September 1825. [CCMA: 21.9.1825]

LILLIAS, master John Bell, from Port Wigtown to Richibucto in September 1827. [NAS.E504.37.7]

LILLIE OF GLASGOW, a brigantine, to the West Indies in 1726. [NAS.AC9.1098]

LILLY OF GLASGOW, master James Bayllie, arrived in Port Glasgow on 13 October 1742 from Virginia. [NAS.E504.28.1]

LILLY, master James Somerville, arrived in the Rappahannock, Virginia, on 7 February 1753 from Glasgow.[VaGaz#102]

LILLY, master James Lyon, from Greenock via Madeira to the West Indies in January 1770; master Alexander Keith, from

Port Glasgow to New York in August 1777,
[NAS.E504.28.27][CM#7404]

LILLY OF BO'NESS, master Hercules Angus, from Bo'ness to
Charleston, South Carolina, in September 1770. [CM#7555]

LITTLE JOHN, Captain Paterson, from Greenock to Boston,
Massachusetts, in August 1802, sailed 2 September 1802
bound for Wiscasset, Maine. [GA#1/65, 70]

LITTLE WILLIAM, master John Murray, from Leith in June 1758
bound for Jamaica and Virginia. [NAS.E504.22.8]

LIVERPOOL PACKET, an American ship, master Isaac Waite,
from Greenock to New York in September 1802. [GA#1/67]

LOIS, from Port Glasgow to Quebec and Montreal in August 1829.
[NAS.E504.28.149]

LORD BYRON, Captain Robinson, arrived in Quebec during July
1827 *with 26 passengers* from Greenock. [QM: 21.7.1827];
from Port Glasgow to St John, New Brunswick, in August
1829. [NAS.E504.28.149]

LORD CRANSTOUN, Captain Urquhart, from Inverkeithing to
Jamaica in November 1823. [NAS.E504.16.1]

LORD FREDERICK, master Peter Speir, from Greenock to
Newfoundland in February 1767. [NAS.E504.15.14]

LORD KEITH, from Greenock/Port Glasgow to Montreal in March
1802. [GA#8/26]

LORD MIDDLETON, Captain Kerr, arrived in Quebec on 20 July
1817 *with 130 passengers* from Leith. [MG]

LOUDOUN OF GLASGOW, a galley, master Archibald Yuill,
from Scotland to the Canary Islands in 1705.
[CalSPDom.SP44/392/77]

LOUDOUN, James King, from Greenock to Antigua in December
1764. [NAS.E504.15.12]

LOVELY BETSEY, master Aaron Martine, from Greenock to Grenada in October 1763. [NAS.E504.15.12]

LOVELY MARY, from Annan, Dumfries-shire, to Miramachi, New Brunswick, in April 1817. [DWJ.8.4.1817]

LUCRETIA OF ST KITTS, master James Fleming, from Port Glasgow to St Kitts in March 1748. [NAS.E504.28.3]

LUCY, Captain Greig, from Greenock to Newfoundland on 3 April 1802. [GA#1/26]

LUNE, Captain Fraser, from Leith *with 13 passengers* to Jamaica on 19 January 1823. [LCL.XI.1135]

LUSITANIA OF BOSTON, master John Blany, arrived in Greenock on 22 March 1743 from North Carolina. [NAS.E504.15.1]

LYON, master David Ferguson, was wrecked on the coast of Ireland on the return voyage from Barbados, 1705. [NAS.AC9.164]

LYON OF LEITH, 140 tons, master Robert Mudie, arrived in Hampton, Virginia, in July 1767 from Leith; from Leith to Grenada and Tobago in April 1770; Charles Bruce, from Leith to Grenada in April 1771; Robert Mudie, from Leith to Jamaica and Grenada in March 1773. [VG:16.7.1767] [NAS.E504.22.15/16/18] [CM#7287]

MAC, master W. F. Hill, from Greenock to Charleston, South Carolina, in February 1802, sailed 2 March 1802. [GA#8/17]

MACFARLANE OF GLASGOW, master William Watson, from Greenock *with passengers* to Jamaica in March 1739; arrived in Greenock on 31 January 1741 from Jamaica; from Port Glasgow *with passengers/indentured servants/tradesmen* to Jamaica on 21 April 1741; master James Peadie, arrived in Greenock on 20 February 1742 from Jamaica; from Port Glasgow *with passengers* on 25 April 1742; master Archibald Hamilton, from Greenock to Jamaica in April 1743. [CM#2933/3255/3257/3289/3350/3366][NAS.E504.15.1]

MACKENZIE OF LEITH, Eugene Fotheringham, from Leith to Jamaica on 14 November 1730, [NAS.E508.26.6]; master John Esdale, returned to Leith via Montrose, Angus, in January 1734 from Virginia. [NAS.CE53.1.2]

MAGNET, 350 tons, master Thomas Mitchell, from Leith to New York in June 1822, [EEC#17,303]

MAJESTIC, from Kirkcaldy, Fife, to Quebec in May 1828, [NAS.E504.20.17]; from Dundee to New York in December 1829. [NAS.E504.11.26]

MALLY OF CRAWFORDDYKE later OF GLASGOW, master John Pettigrew, arrived in Fort William, Inverness-shire, from Virginia in 1740; from Greenock to Virginia on 2 May 1741; master William Dunlop, arrived in Greenock on 23 June 1741 from Virginia; from Greenock to Virginia on 25 July 1741; arrived in Greenock on 28 November 1741 from Virginia; from Greenock to Virginia on 23 March 1742; master Hugh Wallace, from Greenock to Virginia on 1 May 1742; master William Dunlop, arrived in Port Glasgow on 27 October 1742 from Virginia. [CM#3217/3293/3317/3332/3313/3361/3378] [NAS.E504.26.1]

MALLY OF GLASGOW, 150 tons, master John Douglas, from Leith to St Kitts in January 1757. [NAS.E504.22.7]

MALLY, master Robert Bennet, arrived in the James River, Virginia, on 22 August 1768 from Glasgow. [VG:1.9.1768]

MALLY OF DUMFRIES, from Kirkcudbright to Halifax, Nova Scotia, in 1776, captured by an American privateer but later liberated by the British in 1777. [NAS.AC7.60]

MANCHESTER, a brig, Captain Hutcheson, from Leith to Halifax, Nova Scotia, in March 1822. [EEC#17257]

MARCHIONESS OF HUNTLY, Captain Thompson, arrived in Quebec on 5 June 1820 from Aberdeen. [QM]

MARGARET OF GLASGOW, master Archibald Campbell, from Port Glasgow to Antigua in December 1709; returned from Virginia to the Clyde in 1711; master William Rodger, from

Port Glasgow to Antigua in February 1714, [NAS.E508.3.6;
E508.7.6][SC: 1.8.1711]

MARGARET OF LEITH, master Ebenezer Hathorn, to the West
Indies in 1718. [NAS.AC9.626]

MARGARET, master Hugh Crawford, from the Clyde to Virginia
in 1735. [GHG#210]

MARGARET, a brig, master Robert Miller, from Greenock to
Halifax, Nova Scotia, in February 1802, also on 18 September
1802. [GA#1/7, 74]

MARGARET OF PETERHEAD, master J. Shand, from Leith
with 16 passengers bound for Quebec in July 1815.
[NAS.E504.22.70]

MARGARET OF PERTH, master Robert Barclay, from Dundee
with 4 passengers bound for Jamaica on 19 December 1815.
[NAS.CE70.1.4.198]

MARGARET, master William Brodie, arrived in Quebec on 22
May 1819 from Peterhead. [MG:2.6.1819]

MARGARET, Captain Oliphant, from Leith on 16 June 1820 *with
60 passengers* bound for Quebec, arrived there on 10 August
1820; arrived in Quebec during June 1821 *with 180
passengers* from Greenock; Captain Boyd, from Greenock on
18 July 1825 *with 22 passengers* bound for Quebec, arrived
there on 4 September 1825; arrived in Quebec during August
1826 *with 55 passengers* from Greenock. [MG]
[QM:18.6.1821/5.8.1826][CCMA:10.9.1825]

MARGARET, a brig, master James Aitken, arrived in Quebec on
13 June 1821 from Leith; Captain Ferguson, from Dundee on
2 August 1822 *with 5 passengers* bound for Quebec, arrived
there on 12 October 1822; Captain Troup, from Leith on 2
April 1823 *with 2 passengers* bound for Quebec, arrived there
on 20 May 1823; from Leith on 11 August 1823, arrived in
Quebec on 26 September 1823; from Inverkeithing to
Montreal in March 1824, arrived there on 18 May 1824;
Captain Smith, arrived in Quebec on 30 July 1824 from Leith;
Captain Troup, from Leith *with 2 passengers* bound for

Quebec, arrived there on 24 September 1824; from Leith on 3
April 1825 *with passengers* bound for Quebec, arrived there
on 19 May 1825; from Leith on 24 August 1825 *with
passengers* bound for Quebec, arrived there on 11 October
1825; from Aberdeen on 29 April 1826 bound for Quebec,
arrived there on 6 June 1826; from Inverkeithing to Quebec in
June 1828. [MG: 20.6.1821; 19.10.1822; 12.5.1824]
[CC:24.5.1823; 1.10.1823; 4.8.1824; 29.9.1824]
[NAS.E504.16.1][CCMA: 25.5.1825; 15.10.1825; 10.6.1826]

MARGARET, Captain Hughan, from Dumfries on 25 August 1824,
arrived on 10 October 1824. [CC.16.10.1824]

MARGARET OF CAMPBELTOWN, master Robert McMillan,
from Campbeltown, Argyll, to Chaleur Bay, New Brunswick,
on 27 April 1825. [NAS.E504.8.10]

MARGARET, from Kirkcaldy, Fife, to Quebec in March 1828.
[NAS.E504.20.17]

MARGARET BALFOUR, from Dundee to Quebec in August
1829. [NAS.E504.11.26]

MARGARET BOGLE, Captain Boyd, arrived in Quebec *with 17
passengers* from Glasgow during June 1824. [QM:16.6.1824]

MARGARET POLLOCK, Captain McArthur, from Glasgow on 7
April 1825 bound for Quebec, arrived there on 16 May; from
Dundee to St John, New Brunswick, in October 1829.
[CCMA.21.5.1825][NAS.E504.11.26]

MARGARET RITCHIE, from Irvine, Ayrshire, to Dalhousie, New
Brunswick, in September 1828; from Irvine to Dalhousie in
August 1829. [NAS.E504.18.20]

MARIA, Captain Jamieson, from Port Glasgow to Kingston,
Jamaica, in July 1802. [GA#1/51]

MARIANNE, master D. Thompson, arrived in Quebec during
September 1819 from Greenock. [MG.27.9.1819]

MARIE OF BOSTON, master James Smith, from Port Glasgow to
Fyall in September 1689; master William Black, arrived in

Port Glasgow on 27 February 1691 from Maryland. [NAS.E72.19.15/21]

MARIE OF ST MARY'S, MARYLAND, master William Black, from Port Glasgow to the West Indies on 24 September 1691. [NAS.E72.19.22]

MARINER, Captain Briggs, from Dundee to North America, 1 April 1823. [DPCA#1079]

MARION OF GLASGOW, later OF GOUROCK, a 70 ton brigantine, master William Maccunn, from Greenock *with passengers* to Boston, New England, in June 1741, sailed 1 August 1741; from Greenock to Boston on 27 February 1742; arrived in Greenock on 5 January 1743 from Boston. [CM#3306/3333/3330/3351][NAS.E504.15.1]

MARJORY, master William Boyle, from Bo'ness to Jamaica, 1734. [NAS.AC10.194]

MARJORY PACKET OF MONTROSE, master John Spence, returned to Montrose on 12 October 1732 from Virginia. [NAS.CE53.1.1/2]

MARS, master James Weir, from Port Glasgow *with passengers* to St Kitts and Guadaloupe on 6 October 1750; from Greenock to St Kitts in October 1758. [AJ#665][NAS.E504.15.9]

MARS, a US brig, Captain Lord, from Greenock to Baltimore on 10 July 1824. [DPCA#1143]

MARTHA OF GLASGOW, master William Dunlop, arrived in Port Glasgow in November 1734 from Virginia, [NAS.E512/1455]; master James Gregory, from the Clyde to Virginia in 1735, arrived in Port Glasgow on 15 January 1736 from Virginia. [GHG#210][NAS.E512/1455]

MARTHA, a brig, Captain Denwood, from Dumfries to Quebec and Montreal in May 1820; arrived in Quebec on 31 August 1820 *with 34 passengers* from Dumfries; Captain Kennedy, from Troon on 6 April 1822 bound for Quebec, arrived there on 2 June 1822. [DWJ.30.5.1820][QM:8.6.1822]

MARTHA AND SALLY OF MONTROSE, a brigantine, master William Wilkie, in the York River, Virginia, in July 1738. [VG#105]

MARY OF BOSTON, master James Smith, arrived in Port Glasgow in July 1689 from Virginia. [NAS.E72.19.14]

MARY OF GLASGOW, master Robert McCleirie, from Greenock to Barbados in February 1710 and in December 1715, [NAS.E508.9.6/10.6]

MARY OF WHITEHAVEN, master William Whiteside, from the Rappahannock River, Virginia, to Glasgow in 1716. [NAS.AC13.1.160]

MARY OF MONTROSE, master James Stratton, returned to Montrose, Angus, on 5 October 1727 from Philadelphia; from Montrose on 8 February 1728 to Maryland. [NAS.CE53.1.1]

MARY OF INVERNESS, master David Tolmie, from Inverness to Virginia in 1729. [NAS.AC10.151]

MARY OF LEITH, master William Graham, from Leith *with 20 servants* to Jamaica in 1730. [NAS.AC9.1509]

MARY OF PHILADELPHIA, a brigantine, master John Symms, from Philadelphia via Virginia to Dunbar, and return via Lisbon to Philadelphia, 1731. [NAS.AC9.1159]

MARY OF GLASGOW, master Archibald Crawford, from Greenock via the Isle of Maia bound for Virginia in September 1740; arrived in Leith in August 1741 from Virginia. [CM#3316/3333]

MARY OF DUNBARTON, master William Butcher, arrived in Greenock on 27 December 1740 from Virginia; master John Bain, from Greenock to Virginia on 1 May 1742; arrived in Greenock on 7 March 1743 from Maryland. [CM#3240/3378] [NAS.E504.15.1]

MARY, master Robert Simson, from Greenock to St Kitts in December 1764. [NAS.E504.15.12]

MARY OF DUNDEE, PB, 130 tons, master John Ireland, from Dundee via Madeira and the Canary Islands to Jamaica in April 1768. [NAS.E504.11.6]

MARY OF LEITH, 100 tons, master Robert Speirs, from Leith to Jamaica in October 1770, *'Wanted, one mason, one wright, and a blacksmith'* ; November 1771 and in November 1772; master Andrew Mason, from Kirkcaldy, Fife, and Leith to Jamaica in September 1773, [NAS.E504.20.8; E504.22.16/17/18][CM#7563]

MARY, master James Kelso, from Greenock to City Point, James River, Virginia, in February 1802. [GA#14]

MARY, 200 tons, master William H. Nichols, from Greenock to New York in March 1802. [GA#15]

MARY, a 120 ton brig, master Thomas Jones, from Greenock to Halifax, Nova Scotia, and St John, New Brunswick, in August 1802. [GA#1/52]

MARY, Captain Moore, from Greenock in April 1817 *with 18 passengers* bound for Quebec, arrived there on 31 May 1817; Captain Penrice, arrived in Quebec on 11 June 1818 *with 12 passengers* from Greenock . [MG: 9.6.1817; 1.7.1818]

MARY, master John Innes, arrived in Quebec on 22 May 1819 from Peterhead. [MG:2.6.1819]

MARY, Captain Munro, arrived in Quebec on 31 May 1819 *with 32 passengers* from Leith; master John Jacobson, arrived in Quebec on 6 September 1819 from Leith. [MG:9.6.1819; 15.9.1819]

MARY, from Greenock *with passengers* to New Orleans, arrived there on 21 December 1821. [NARA.M259/2]

MARY, Captain Dunlop, arrived in Quebec during May 1828 *with 206 passengers* from Greenock; arrived in Quebec during May 1829 *with 161 passengers* from Greenock. [QM:31.5.1828/30.5.1829]

MARY, a bark, Captain Dawson, from Leith on 2 April 1825 bound for Quebec, arrived there on 17 May 1825; from Leith to Halifax, Nova Scotia, in July 1829. [CCMA: 21.5.1825] [NAS.E504.22.128]

MARY AND BETTY, 140 tons, master James Melven, from Aberdeen *with passengers* to Antigua on 21 March 1749. [AJ#54/64]

MARY AND FRANCES OF WHITEHAVEN, possibly from Glasgow to Maryland and Virginia in 1725. [NAS.AC8.498; AC8.310]

MARY AND JEAN OF GREENOCK, master Daniel Rodger, when bound for North Carolina, was wrecked on South Uist on 6 February 1741. [CM#3273]

MARY AND SUSAN, from Greenock *with passengers* bound for New York, arrived there on 5 August 1828. [NARA.M237/12]

MARY ANN, Captain Inglis, from Greenock to Charleston on 29 April 1802. [GA#1/34]

MARY ANN, master J. Lawson, arrived in Quebec on 13 May 1820 from Aberdeen; master J. Moore, arrived in Quebec on 8 October 1820 from Aberdeen; arrived in Quebec on 15 May 1821 *with 6 passengers* from Aberdeen; from Aberdeen on 31 August 1821 bound for Quebec, arrived there on 15 October 1821; from Aberdeen on 26 August 1822 bound for Quebec, arrived there on 17 October 1822. [QM][MG:31.10.1821; 23.10.1822]

MARY'S ALBION, 103 tons, master John Moyes, arrived in Prince Edward Island on 24 May 1809 from Kirkcaldy, Fife. [PAPEI.RG9]

MASTERTON, from Dysart on 5 June 1822, arrived in Quebec on 5 June 1822. [MG:12.6.1822]

MATILDA, a schooner, master Malcolm Dugald, from the Clyde to Demerara, Martinique, St Vincent, and Trinidad, 1796-1797. [NAS.AC7.73]

MATTIE OF GLASGOW, master James Hume, arrived in Port
Glasgow on 27 November 1742 from Virginia.
[NAS.E504.28.1]

MATTY, a sloop, master James Gregory, from Port Glasgow to
Barbados in February 1743; from Port Glasgow to Jamaica in
September 1743. [NAS.E504.28.1]

MAXWELL, a brig, from Kirkcudbright to Grenada in 1788.
[DWJ.16.12.1788]

MAY OF GREENOCK, master William Dunlop, arrived in Port
Glasgow in December 1734 from Virginia. [NAS.E512/1455]

MAY OF GLASGOW, master Alexander Stirling, arrived in the
James River, Virginia, via Boston on 24 June 1738; arrived in
the James River, Virginia, in 1739 from Glasgow; arrived in
Greenock on 18 September 1740 from Virginia; master
Andrew Turner, from Greenock to Virginia on 14 March
1741; arrived in Greenock on 10 October 1741 from Virginia;
arrived in Greenock on 22 May 1742 from Virginia; arrived in
Greenock on 5 January 1743 from Boston; arrived in the
James River, Virginia, in the Fall of 1744; master John Orr,
arrived in the Upper District of the James River, Virginia, on
6 May 1745 from Greenock. [VaGaz#106/158/466]
[CM#3197/3273/3363/3387][NAS.E504.15.1]

MAYFLOWER OF GLASGOW, master Thomas Stalker, arrived
in Glasgow on 10 March 1686 from the West Indies.
[NAS.E72.19.12]

MAYFLOWER OF LONDON, master Thomas Mooch, arrived in
Port Glasgow in August 1689 from Maryland.
[NAS.E72.19.14]

MAYFLOWER OF GLASGOW, master Robert Jameson, from
Greenock to Barbados in October 1716, [NAS.E508.10.6]

MAYFLOWER OF WHITEHAVEN, master Edward Tubman, to
Virginia by 1727. [NAS.AC9.976]

MEARNS, from Port Glasgow to Miramachi, New Brunswick, in July 1829. [NAS.E504.28.149]

MENNY, master Alexander Thomson, from Greenock to Guadaloupe in May 1762. [NAS.E504.15.11]

MENIE, Captain McKellar, from Port Glasgow to St John's in the St Laurence in June 1802. [GA#1/50]

MENTOR, master Josiah L. Wilson, from Greenock *with passengers* to New York on 10 August 1824. [DPCA#1145]

MERCURY OF IRVINE, from Greenock to Virginia on 24 July 1740. [CM#3172]

MERCURY OF SALTCOATS later OF GLASGOW, a 70 ton brigantine, master Henry Laird, arrived in Greenock on 28 March 1741 from Virginia; from Port Glasgow to Boston, New England, on 27 February 1742; master John McCall, from Port Glasgow to Jamaica and Barbados in December 1746. [CM#3279/3331/3351][NAS.E504.28.3]

MERCURY OF DUNDEE, 90 tons, master James Strachan, from Dundee to Charleston, South Carolina, on 12 July 1753; from Leith to South Carolina in June 1754. [NAS.E504.11.3//22.6]

MERCURY OF MONTROSE, master Robert Mudie, arrived in Aberdeen on 15 February 1753 from Virginia. [NAS.E504.1.4]

MERCURY, master James Malcolm, from Greenock to Jamaica in October 1767. [NAS.E504.15.15]

MERCURY, a 200 ton American ship, master Michael Beath, from Greenock to New York in February 1802, sailed 6 March 1802. [GA#6/17]

MERCURY, Captain Edington, from Greenock to Newfoundland on 25 April 1802. [GA#1/30]

MERRYMAKE OF BOSTON, a brigantine, arrived in Greenock on 7 April 1741 from Boston; from Port Glasgow *with* *passengers* to Boston, New England, in May 1741. [CM#3283/3292]

MERSEY, Captain Grindlay, arrived in Quebec on 8 July 1826 from Leith. [CCMA: 12.7.1826]

MIDAS, a brig, Captain Mawer, from Dundee on 1 July 1824 *with 4 passengers* bound for Quebec, arrived there on 1 September 1824; from Dundee on 20 March 1825 bound for Quebec, arrived there on 17 May 1825; from Dundee in August 1825 bound for Quebec, arrived there on 19 October 1825; from Dundee in April 1826 bound for Quebec, arrived there on 15 May 1826. [CC.8.9.1824] [CCMA: 21.5.1825; 26.10.1825; 20.5.1826]

MINERVA, 300 tons, master William Gibbon, from Aberdeen to Grenada and Tobago *with passengers* in January 1775. [AJ#1400]

MINERVA, Captain Anderson, from Port Glasgow to St Vincent in April 1802. [GA#1/26]

MINERVA, a brig, Captain Williamson, arrived in Quebec on 30 June 1820 *with 60 passengers* from Greenock; from Greenock *with passengers* bound for New York, arrived there on 29 October 1822; Captain John C. Mayell, from Greenock *with passengers* to New York on 10 September 1824; Captain Williamson, from Leith *with passengers* bound for Quebec on 20 April 1825, arrived there on 25 May 1825.[MG] [NARA.M237/3] [DPCA#1143] [CCMA:1.6.1825]

MIRAMACHI, from Port Glasgow to St John, New Brunswick, in August 1829. [NAS.E504.28.149]

MOLLY OF GLASGOW, master Colin Dunlop, arrived in the James River, Virginia, in 1739 from Glasgow; from Glasgow on 3 November 1739, arrived at Hampton, Virginia, on 10 January 1740; arrived in Greenock on 12 August 1740 from Virginia; master William Dunlop, from Greenock to Virginia on 4 October 1740. [VG:4.5.1739][CM#3181/3204][VaGaz#180]

MOLLY OF CRAWFORDDYKE, master James Calhoun, arrived in Hampton, Virginia, on 10 May 1745 from Glasgow. [VG#460]

MONARCH, Captain Crawford, from Greenock on 19 August 1822 bound for Quebec, arrived there on 30 September 1822; arrived in Quebec on 17 August 1823 *with 259 passengers* from Tobermory, Mull, Argyll, on 9 July 1823. [MG.5.10.1822] [QM:19.8.1823][MH:23.8.1823]

MONTEZUMA, master Thomas Morgan, from Greenock to Charleston, South Carolina, in August 1802. [GA#1/57]

MONTGOMERY OF IRVINE, master James Montgomery, from Greenock to Virginia on 25 July 1741; arrived in Greenock on 6 February 1742 from Virginia; arrived in Port Glasgow on 3 February 1743 from Virginia. [CM#3332/3343][NAS.E504.28.1]

MONTGOMERY, master Alexander Montgomery, from Greenock to Barbados in August 1763. [NAS.E504.15.11]

MONTREAL, master William Raeside, from Greenock on 9 April 1817 *with 10 passengers* bound for Quebec, arrived there on 29 May 1817; Captain Service, arrived in Quebec on 2 June 1818 *with 8 passengers* from Greenock. [MG: 2.6.1817; 10.6.1818]

MONTROSE, master Robert Paisley, arrived in Virginia during June 1739 from Glasgow; master Andrew Crawford, from Greenock to Jamaica on 17 January 1741; master James Gregory, from Port Glasgow to Antigua in March 1743; from Port Glasgow to Antigua in March 1744. [VaGaz#170][CM#3249][NAS.E504.28.1]

MOSES GILL, Captain Paterson, from Greenock to New York in May 1802. [GA#1/35]

MURDOCH, master Archibald Orr, arrived in Virginia during September 1769 from Greenock. [NA.AO12.35.1]

NANCY OF ABERDEEN, master James Park, from Aberdeen to Maryland on 8 April 1748. [NAS.E504.1.2]

NANCY OF BURNTISLAND, 80 tons, master Alexander Ritchie, from Kirkcaldy, Fife, to Charleston, South Carolina, on 27 September 1753. [NAS.E504.20.3]

NANCY, master Andrew Anderson, from Greenock to Antigua in December 1764; from Greenock to Antigua in October 1765; master William Gilkison, from Greenock to Grenada in October 1767. [NAS.E504.15.12/13/15]

NANCY OF LEITH, 140 tons, master Robert Millar, from Leith to Tobago in March 1773; from Leith in March 1775 bound for Tobago and Grenada from St Kitts to London, pre 1781. [NAS.E504.22.18/19; AC7.58]

NANCY, master William Gilkison, from Greenock to Grenada and Antigua in December 1766; from Port Glasgow to Grenada in October 1774 and in October 1775. [NAS.E504.15.14; E504.28.24/25]

NANCY, master John Steele, from Port Glasgow to Jamaica in January 1776. [NAS.E504.28.25]

NANCY, 346 tons, master Nicol Baine, from Greenock to Quebec in March 1802. [GA#8]

NANCY, Captain Scott, from Inverkeithing to Jamaica in November 1826. [NAS.E504.16.1]

NANNIO OF PORT GLASGOW, from Glasgow to South Carolina and return via Fife, Scotland, to Hamburg, Bremen or Amsterdam, 1728. [NAS.AC7.34.697; AC8.250]

NEIL, from Greenock on 19 August 1824 *with 10 passengers* bound for Quebec, arrived there on 11 October 1824. [CC.16.10.1824]

NELLY OF GLASGOW, master Ninian Bryce, from the Clyde to Virginia in 1735, arrived in Port Glasgow on 29 December 1735 from Virginia. [GHG#210][NAS.E512/1455; master John Somervill, arrived in Glasgow in September 1740 from St Kitts; from Greenock to St Kitts on 27 December 1740; master Archibald Hamilton, arrived in Greenock on 26 May

1741 from St Kitts; from Greenock to St Kitts on 25 July 1741; arrived in Greenock on 9 January 1742 from St Kitts; master John Lyon, from Greenock to St Kitts on 3 April 1742. [CM#3316/3240/3305/3332/3329/3367]

NELLY OF GLASGOW, arrived in Virginia on 3 April 1771, via Barbados. [VSS#177]

NELLY OF MONTROSE, 100 tons, master James Webster, from Kirkcaldy, Fife, to Grenada in January 1772, [NAS.E504.20.8]

NELLY, master Angus McLarty, from Greenock to St Kitts in November 1762; John Wilson, from Greenock to Barbados in December 1766. [NAS.E504.15.11/14]

NELSON, master Alexander Smith, from Greenock to Trinidad on 12 February 1802. [GA#9]

NELSON, Captain Barwick, arrived in Quebec during September 1819 *with 19 passengers* from Leith.[MG.27.9.1819]

NEPTUNE, from Glasgow to Boston, New England, 1728. [NAS.CS96.3814]
NEPTUNE, master Robert Hamilton, from the Clyde to Jamaica in 1735. [GHG#210]

NEPTUNE OF GLASGOW, master Robert Brock, from Virginia, was wrecked on Bute on 15 January 1742. [CM#3335]

NEPTUNE OF AYR, master Robert Allan, from Ayr to Falmouth, New England, in 1767. [NAS.E504.4.4]

NEPTUNE, master Robert McLeish, from Irvine, Ayrshire, to Montserrat in May 1767. [NAS.E504.18.6]

NEPTUNE, master John Malcolm, from Greenock to Port Morant, Jamaica, in January 1802, sailed 5 February. [GA#2/8]

NEPTUNE, master James Neil, from Greenock to Quebec in March 1802, sailed 14 April 1802. [GA#20/29]; Captain Neil, from Greenock on 16 April 1817 *with 22 passengers* bound for Quebec, arrived there on 9 June 1817. [MG:9.6.1817]

NEPTUNE, Captain Boyd, from Greenock *with passengers* to Quebec in May 1802, arrived there in September 1802. [GA#1/41][QGaz.11.9.1802]

NEPTUNE, a brig, Captain Clark, from Glasgow on 16 April 1817 *with 5 passengers* bound for Quebec, arrived there on 6 June 1817; arrived in Quebec on 19 May 1818 *with 34 passengers* from Glasgow. [MG: 9.6.1817]

NEPTUNE, Captain Bell, from Leith on 19 April 1821 *with 53 passengers* bound for Quebec, arrived there on 6 June 1821. [MG.13.6.1821]

NEREID OF DUMFRIES, from Wigtown to Richibucto, New Brunswick, in June 1829, also in August 1829. [NAS.E504.37.7]

NEREOUS, master Robert Wilson, arrived in Quebec on 18 May 1819 *with 53 passengers* from Glasgow. [MG:26.5.1819]

NESTOR, Captain Thom, from Aberdeen on 16 May 1822 *with 5 passengers* bound for Quebec, arrived there on 7 July 1822. [MG.13.7.1822]

NEW SNOW, a brig, from Dumfries to Boston, Massachusetts, in May 1817. [DWJ.13.5.1817]

NEW SUPPLY OF CHESTER, master John Glover, from Glasgow to America in March 1684. [NAS.E72.19.12]

NIAGARA, a brig, Captain Hamilton, from Greenock *with 268 passengers from Perthshire* bound for Montreal and Quebec, arrived in Quebec on 18 May 1825. [CCMA: 25.5.1825; 28.5.1825]

NIGHTINGALE OF HULL, master John Hobson, arrived in Kirkcaldy, Fife, on 17 May 1673 from 'Wayrter' in Virginia or Maryland. [NAS.E72.9.8/2]

NIGHTINGALE OF WHITEHAVEN, from Greenock to Virginia on 25 November 1715. [GCt#2]; to Virginia in 1726. [NAS.AC10.137; AC7.34.433; AC9.1056]

NILE, arrives in Miramichi, New Brunswick, in 1817 from Dumfries. [DWJ.5.8.1817]

NORTH STAR, a schooner, from Dumfries and Urr, Dumfries-shire, to North America in 1817. [DWJ.18.2.1817]

NORTHERN FRIENDS, Captain Montgomery, from Greenock to Cape Breton in May 1802. [GA#1/37]

NORTHUMBERLAND, Captain Davison, from Glasgow on 8 April 1824 *with passengers* bound for Quebec, arrived there on 3 June 1824. [MG:9.6.1824]

NORVAL, a brig, Captain D. Walker, from Aberdeen on 27 June 1818 *with 3 passengers* bound for Quebec, arrived there on 23 August 1818; arrived in Quebec on 13 May 1820 from Aberdeen. [MG]

ORION, master William Graden, from Greenock on 10 September 1819 *with 1 passenger* bound for Quebec, arrived there on 29 October 1819. [MG.10.11.1819]

OSPREY, from Greenock to Charleston in October 1829. [NAS.E504.15.170]

OSSIAN OF LEITH, a 194 ton brig, J. Black, arrived in Quebec on 23 August 1822 *with 127 passengers* from Fort William, Inverness-shire, on 5 July 1822; from Greenock to New York in 1822. [QM:28.8.1822][L]

OUGHTON, a sailing snow, Captain McClure, from Greenock to Quebec on 7 April 1802. [GA#17/27]

OWNER'S GOODWILL OF ARBROATH, Charles Kenny, from Kirkcaldy, Fife, to Tobago and Grenada in February 1772. [NAS.E504.20.8]

OXFORD, from Port Glasgow to Quebec in July 1829. [NAS.E504.28.149]

PAGE, master John Smith, from Ayr to Madeira and Jamaica in April 1751. [NAS.E504.4.2]

PAISLEY OF PAISLEY, master William Houston, from Greenock via Ireland to Virginia on 1 August 1741. [CM#3333]

PALLAS, master James Noble, from Greenock to New York and Philadelphia in Septmber 1770. [CM#7563]

PALLAS, a 178 ton brig, Captain Bowden, from Greenock to Charleston on 6 March 1802; master T. Booth, from Greenock to New Brunswick in 1821. [GA#17][L]

PANDORA, Captain Galt, from Greenock to Newfoundland in June 1802. [GA#1/48]

PARAGON, master Thomas Mitchell, arrived in Quebec *with 66 passengers* from Leith on 30 August 1819. [QM: 31.8.1819] [MG:8.9.1819]

PASTORA OF WIGTOWN, master Robert Whitehead, from Wigtown to St John, New Brunswick, in April 1828, from Wigtown to Quebec in August 1828, also from Wigtown to St John, New Brunswick, in April 1829, and in July 1829 from Wigtown to Quebec. [NAS.E504.37.7; E504.9.10]

PATRIOT, a brig, master Alexander Anderson, from Aberdeen on 29 March 1817 bound for Quebec, arrived there on 29 May 1817; arrived in Quebec on 22 September 1817 from Greenock; arrived in Quebec on 7 May 1818 *with 6 passengers* from Aberdeen; arrived in Quebec on 1 May 1819 *with passengers* from Aberdeen; from Aberdeen on 8 August 1819, arrived in Quebec on 25 September 1819; master J. Troop, arrived in Quebec on 11 May 1820 *with 9 passengers* from Aberdeen; arrived in Quebec on 15 May 1821 from Aberdeen. [MG: 2.6.1817; 1.10.1817; 12.5.1819; 6.10.1819; 23.5.1821] [QM]

PEARL OF WHITEHAVEN, 160 tons, master Thomas Walker, from Glasgow to Virginia, 1724. [NAS.AC9.868]

PEARL, master ...Tucker, arrived in New York during October 1773 *with 280 passengers* from Fort William. [VG: 11.11.1773]

PEGGIE OF LEITH, 80 tons, master Alexander Matheson, from Leith to Grenada in January 1771; master Dougal Matheson, from Kirkcaldy, Fife, to Tobago in December 1771; Thomas Hogg, from Leith to Tobago in November 1772. [NAS.E504.20.8; E504.22.16/17]

PEGGY OF GLASGOW, master William Walkinshaw, arrived in Greenock on 28 November 1741 from Virginia; from Greenock to Virginia on 23 March 1742; arrived in Port Glasgow on 9 October 1742 from Virginia. [CM#3313/3361] [NAS.E504.28.1]

PEGGY, master William Dunlop, from Greenock to Antigua in October 1758; master david Andrew, arrived in the James River, Virginia, on 16 May 1760 from Greenock; John Wood, from Greenock to Havannah in December 1762; from Greenock to Montserrat in October 1763; James MacAulay, from Greenock to Jamaica in December 1764. [NAS.E504.15.9/11/12][VG:30.5.1760]

PEGGY, a snow, Robert Caldwell, arrived in Boston, Massachusetts, during October 1770 from Glasgow. [BoNL#3492]

PEGGY OF GREENOCK, 120 tons, master Archibald Fisher, from Leith to the Mosquito Shore in November 1770. [NAS.E504.22.16]

PEGGY, a brigantine, Captain Ritchie, from Glasgow *with 18 passengers to settle in Pictou,* bound for Nova Scotia, 1785. [NSARM]

PEGGY, Captain Barclay, from Greenock to Tobago on 10 February 1802. [GA#9]

PEGGY AND NELLY, master Robert Haggart, from Ayr to Jamaica in October 1756. [NAS.E504.4.3]

PEGGY GRAY, from Aberdeen to Newfoundland on 19 March 1777. [AJ#1524]

PENELOPE, master John Chisholm, arrived in Quebec on 18 May 1821 *with 62 passengers* from Glasgow; arrived in Quebec on

20 September 1829 *with 70 passengers* from Glasgow.
[QM][MG.23.5.1821]

PERCIVAL, master John Scott, arrived in Quebec on 26 May 1819
with 85 passengers from Leith; from Inverkeithing to New
York in March 1820; from Inverkeithing to New York in
April 1821; from Inverkeithing to Charlestown in December
1822; Captain Johnston, from Inverkeithing via Leith to
Montreal and Quebec in April 1826, arrived there on 23 May
1826. [MG:2.6.1819][NAS.E504.16.1][CCMA:27.5.1826]

PERCIVAL OF LEITH, Captain Johnson, arrived in Quebec
during May 1827 *with 47 passengers* from Leith. [QM:
19.5.1827]

PHOENIX OF DUNDEE, master James Maxwell, arrived in
Dundee on 25 June 1755 from Madeira. [NAS.E504.11.3]

PHOENIX, master ... Lamont, from Glasgow bound for Virginia
when stranded in the Capes on 12 December 1772. [VG]

PILGRIM, Captain Smith, arrived in Quebec on 23 August 1822
with 62 passengers from Tobermory, Mull, Argyll, on 14
June 1822; arrived in Quebec on 11 August 1823 *with 77
passengers* from Greenock on 25 June 1823.
[QM:28.8.1822/12.8.1823][CC:16.8.1823]

PILOT, master John Law, from Aberdeen on 1 April 1819, arrived
in Quebec on 7 May 1819; from Aberdeen on 26 June 1823,
arrived in Quebec on 13 August 1823; from Aberdeen on 31
March 1824, arrived in Quebec on 2 June 1824.
[MG:19.5.1819; 9..6.1824] [MH:20.8.1823]

PINK OF BOSTON, arrived in Greenock on 12 March 1741 from
Boston, New England. [CM#3273]

PINKY SLOOP, master Robert Lees, from Port Glasgow *with
indentured servants, joiners, masons and blacksmiths* to
Jamaica in April 1741. [CM#3277]

PITT, master J. Hamilton, from Greenock *with 15 passengers*
bound for Quebec, arrived there on 24 September 1817; from

Irvine, Ayrshire, to Dalhousie, New Brunswick, in July 1828. [MG:1.10.1817][NAS.E504.18.20]

PLANTER OF VIRGINIA, master James Elphinstone, from Aberdeen to Antigua in February 1751. [NAS.E504.1.3]

PLANTER OF ABERDEEN, Captain Ogilvie, from Cromarty on 1 October 1754 *with 80 passengers*, arrived in Antigua on 1 December 1754. [AJ#369]

POLLY, a brig, master A. Donaldson, arrived in Quebec on 18 May 1818 from Leith. [MG]

PORT GLASGOW, master David Blair, from the Clyde to Virginia in 1735. [GHG#210]

PRESIDENT OF GLASGOW, master Thomas Bogle, from Glasgow to Virginia, 1750. [NAS.AC9.1746]

PRESCOTT OF LEITH, Captain Young, arrived in Quebec during June 1816 *with passengers* from Leith. [QM: 21.6.1816]

PRETTY BETSY OF GLASGOW, master John Scott, from Port Glasgow to Jamaica in April 1745; master Andrew Gray, from Greenock to St Kitts in April 1746; from Port Glasgow to St Kitts, 1747. [NAS.E504.28.2/3; E504.15.2]

PRINCE CHARLES OF BELFAST, master Robert Stout, from Campbeltown, Argyll, on 30 April 1745 to Jamaica; master James Egger, from Campbeltown to Kingston, Jamaica, on 27 October 1746. [NAS.E504.8.1]

PRINCE GEORGE, Captain Duncanson, from Leith *with 6 passengers* to Miramachi, New Brunswick, on 7 March 1823. [LCL.XI.1054]

PRINCE OF ASTURIAS, Captain Donnell, from Greenock in April 1817 *with 60 passengers* bound for Quebec, arrived there on 3 June 1817. [MG:9.6.1817]

PRINCE OF COBOURG, master D. Hutchison, arrived in Quebec on 17 May 1819 from Peterhead. [MG:26.5.1819]

PRINCE OF ORANGE OF GLASGOW, master John Andrew, from Greenock to Carolina on 21 April 1741; arrived in Greenock on 16 January 1742 from North Carolina. [CM#3276/3289/3333]

PRINCE OF WALES, master James Gray, from Aberdeen on 1 September 1819, arrived in Quebec on 20 October 1819. [MG.27.10.1819]

PRINCE WILLIAM OF GLASGOW, master James Peadie, from the Clyde to Jamaica in 1735. [GHG#210]; arrived in Greenock on 7 February 1741 from Virginia; master James Butcher, from Greenock to Virginia on 2 May 1741; arrived in Greenock on 10 April 1742 from Virginia. [CM#3258/3293/3369]

PRINCESS ROYAL, Captain Marquis, from the Clyde to Charleston 23 September 1802. [GA#1/75]

PROMPT OF BO'NESS, Captain Coverdale, arrived in Quebec on 6 July 1817 *with 135 passengers* from Greenock, [MG]; master John Kay, arrived in Quebec on 6 May 1819 from Leith; Captain Nairn, arrived in Quebec on 31 August 1820 *with 370 passengers* from Greenock on 4 July 1820. [MG:12.5.1819][QM: 31.8.1820]

PROSPERITY OF GLASGOW, master James Montier, from Glasgow to Virginia, 1732, [NAS.AC9.1354]; master Robert Hunter, from Greenock to Virginia on 3 April 1742, [CM#3367]; master Archibald Galbreith, from Aberdeen to Virginia on 26 December 1746. [NAS.E504.1.2]

PROSPERITY OF AYR, master Adam Doak, from Ayr to Barbados in December 1742; from Ayr via Antigua to Virginia in December 1742. [NAS.E504.4.1]

PROVIDENCE OF GLASGOW, master John Anderson, arrived in Glasgow on 3 September 1672 from Antigua. [NAS.E72.10.3]

PROVIDENCE OF BELFAST, master John Lorimer, arrived in Port Glasgow in September 1689 from Montserrat. [NAS.E72.19.14]

PROVIDENCE OF GLASGOW, 60 tons, master Henry Fisher, arrived in York, Virginia, on 24 April 1727 via Barbados. [VSS#61]

PROVIDENCE OF COLERAINE, master Alexander Doick, arrived in Ayr in July 1786 from Virginia. [NAS.E72.3.16]

PROVIDENCE OF LEITH, 100 tons, Robert Millar, from Leith to Grenada in February 1772. [NAS.E504.22.17]

PROVIDENCE, a brig, Captain Fyffe, arrived in Quebec on 31 July 1817 *with 1 passenger* from Leith. [MG]

PSYCHE, Captain Erskine, arrived in Quebec on 12 May 1819 *with 9 passengers* from Dundee; arrived in Quebec on 27 May 1820 *with 88 passengers* from Dundee, [QM]; master Thomas Macintosh, from Dundee to Quebec and Montreal in October 1822. [MG:19.5.1819][NAS.E504.11.23]

QUEBEC PACKET, Captain A. Anderson, arrived in Quebec on 1 June 1822 *with 10 passengers* from Aberdeen on 20 April 1822; from Aberdeen on 20 August 1822, arrived in Quebec on 1 October 1822; arrived in Quebec on 14 May 1823 *with 10 passengers* from Aberdeen on 8 April 1823; arrived in Quebec on 23 September 1823 *with 16 passengers* from Aberdeen on 5 August 1823; from Aberdeen on 29 March 1824, arrived in Quebec on 7 May 1824; from Aberdeen on 5 August 1824 *with 3 passengers* bound for Quebec, arrived there on 22 September 1824; from Aberdeen on 31 March 1825 bound for Quebec, arrived there on 11 May 1825; from Aberdeen on 20 July 1825 *with 6 passengers* bound for Quebec, arrived there on 12 September 1825; from Aberdeen on 2 April 1826 *with 19 passengers* bound for Quebec, arrived there on 12 May 1826; from Aberdeen to Quebec in July 1826, and also in July 1827. [QM:23.9.1823][NAS.E504.1.32][CC:21.5.1823; 29.9.1824][CCMA: 11.5.1825; 17.9.1825; 17.5.1826] [MG:8.6.1822; 12.5.1824][MH:6.9.1823]

QUEEN ANNE OF WHITEHAVEN, master William Lewis, from Virginia to Glasgow, 1723. [NAS.AC9.862]

QUEEN OF GREENOCK, a 150 ton brigantine, Captain Workman, arrived in Port Brunswick, North Carolina, via St Kitts, on 28 August 1785. [NCSA]

QUEENSBERRY OF DUMFRIES, 85 tons, Thomas Bell, from Leith to Virginia in February 1754, [NAS.E504.22.5]

RACHEL OF LEITH, 90 tons, William Pillans, from Leith to Virginia in August 1754. [NAS.E504.22.6]

RADIANT, a brig, Captain Phillips, arrived in Quebec on 7 July 1826 from Aberdeen. [CCMA:12.7.1826]

RAE GALLEY, from Greenock to Philadelphia, Georgia, Jamaica, the Bay of Honduras, Cork, then Greenock, 1774-1775. [NAS.AC7.55]

RANKIN, from Port Glasgow to St John, New Brunswick, in July 1829. [NAS.E504.28.149]

REBECCA, master A. Harvey, arrived in Quebec on 3 June 1817 *with 29 passengers* from Greenock; arrived in Quebec on 14 May 1818 *with 18 passengers* from Greenock; from Greenock on 6 August 1818 *with 17 passengers* bound for Quebec, arrived there on 9 September 1818; master Thomas McKenzie, arrived in Quebec on 11 May 1819 *with 45 passengers* from Greenock; from Greenock on 19 August 1819 *with 13 passengers* bound for Quebec, arrived there on 28 September 1819; arrived in Quebec on 25 May 1820 *with 42 passengers* from Greenock; arrived in Quebec on 11 October 1820 *with 55 passengers* from Greenock on 28 August 1820; from Greenock on 29 August 1821 *with 19 passengers* bound for Quebec, arrived there on 14 October 1821; from Greenock on 10 April 1822 *with 15 passengers* bound for Quebec, arrived there on 19 May 1822; master A. Harvey, from Greenock on 19 August 1822 *with 19 passengers* bound for Quebec, arrived there on 1 October 1822; arrived in Quebec on 11 May 1823 *with 9 passengers* from Greenock on 10 April 1823; arrived in Quebec on 24 September 1823 *with 25 passengers* from Greenock on 13 August 1823; arrived in Quebec on 31 May 1824 *with 22 passengers* from Greenock on 14 April 1824; from Greenock on 17 April 1825 *with passengers* bound for Quebec, arrived there on 13 May 1825; Captain Laurie, from Greenock on 11 August 1825 *with 4 passengers* bound for Quebec, arrived there on 16 September 1825; from Greenock on 16 April 1826 *with 10 passengers* bound for Quebec, arrived there on 19 May 1826; arrived in Quebec during October 1826 *with 20 passengers* from Greenock; arrived in Quebec during May 1827 *with 20 passengers* from Greenock. [MG: 9.6.1817; 19.5.1819; 6.10.1819; 31.10.1821; 30.5.1822; 9.10.1822; 5.6.1824] [CC.17.5.1823; 1.10.1823] [CCMA: 18.5.1825; 21.9.1825; 24.5.1826] [QM:26.9.1823/1.6.1824/7.10.1826/5.5.1827]

REBECCA AND MARY OF MONTROSE, master George Ouchterlonie, returned to Montrose, Angus, on 22 February 1735 from Virginia and Maryland. [NAS.CE70.1.2]

RECOVERY OF MARYLAND, master Hendry Smith, from Port Glasgow to St George's, (Bermuda), 1691. [NAS.E72.19.22]

RECOVERY, a 169 ton brigantine, master Daniel Campbell, from Greenock *with passengers* to New York in February 1802, sailed 16 March 1802; master R. Bogg, from Greenock to Quebec in 1805. [GA#4/20][L]

REGENT, from Leith to Montreal and Quebec in May 1829. [NAS.E504.22.127]

RENFREW OF RENFREW, master Robert Sommerville, from Greenock to Barbados in November 1728. [NAS.E508.22.6/37, 40]; master Alexander Campbell, arrived in Greenock on 28 March 1741 from Virginia; from Greenock to Virginia on 1 August 1741. [CM#3279/3333]

RENOWN, a brig, Captain Watt, from Leith on 9 April 1817 *with 20 passengers* bound for Quebec, arrived there on 9 June 1817; arrived in Quebec on 9 June 1818 from Leith; from Leith on 12 April 1835 *with 37 passengers* bound for Quebec, arrived there on 17 May 1819; arrived in Quebec on 7 June 1820 *with 13 passengers* from Leith; arrived in Quebec on 18 May 1821 *with 11 passengers* from Leith; from Leith on 25 April 1822 *with 20 passengers* bound for Quebec, arrived there on 4 July 1822; arrived in Quebec on 22 May 1823 from

Leith. [MG: 9.6.1817; 17.6.1818: 26.5.1819; 23.5.1821; 10.7.1822] [CC:28.5.1823]

RESTORATION, master John Shannon, from the Clyde to Boston in 1735. [GHG#210]

RESOLUTION OF GLASGOW, 150 tons, from the Clyde to Jamaica in 1711. [SC: 30.5.1711]

RESOLUTION, a brig, Captain Leishman, arrived in Quebec on 20 May 1819 from Kirkcaldy. [MG:2.6.1819]

RETREAT, from Leith to Miramachi, New Brunswick, in April 1829. [NAS.E504.22.127]; from Grangemouth to Miramachi in August 1829. [NAS.E504.14.10]

REWARD, from Inverkeithing to Jamaica in November 1827. [NAS.E504.16.1]

RISING SUN, from Grangemouth and Leith to Bathurst, New Brunswick, in August 1829. [NAS.E504.22.148; E504.14.10]

ROANOKE OF GREENOCK, a 67 ton sloop, master James Hunter, in North Carolina and Jamaica, 1741. [NAS.AC9.1626]

ROB ROY, a brig, master William Nairn, arrived in Quebec on 13 May 1819 *with 7 passengers* from Aberdeen. [MG:19.5.1819]

ROBERT OF GLASGOW, master Nathaniel Davis, from Port Glasgow to Virginia on 5 March 1691. [NAS.E72.15.22]

ROBERT OF LONDONDERRY, from Glasgow to Virginia in 1691. [NAS.GD3.5.805]

ROBERT, a 140 ton brig, master H.Henry, from Greenock to Jamaica in 1776. [L]

ROBERT, a brig, master J. Neil, arrived in Quebec on 22 July 1817 *with 3 passengers* from Greenock; arrived in Quebec on 4 June 1818 *with 1 passenger* from Glasgow; from Glasgow on 20 August 1819 *with 7 passengers* bound for Quebec, arrived there on 29 October 1819; arrived in Quebec on 21 May 1820

with 45 passengers from Greenock; arrived in Quebec on 11
October 1820 *with 1 passenger* from Greenock; arrived in
Quebec on 18 May 1821 *with 12* passengers from Greenock;
from Glasgow on 31 August 1821 *with 18 passengers* bound
for Quebec, arrived there on 25 October 1821; from Greenock
on 4 April 1822 *with 5 passengers* bound for Quebec, arrived
there on 16 May 1822; from Glasgow on 30 August 1822 *with
22 passengers* bound for Quebec, arrived there on 12 October
1822; from Greenock on 9 April 1823 *with 8 passengers*
bound for Quebec, arrived there on 16 May 1823; from
Greenock on 18 August 1823, arrived in Quebec on 26
September 1823. [MG: 10.6.1818; 27.10.1819; 23.5.1821;
31.10.1821; 30.5.1822; 19.10.1822] [CC:21.5.1823;
1.10.1823]

ROBERT AND ANN OF PORTWILLIAM, master Thomas
Cumming, from Stranraer to St Andrews, New Brunswick, on
30 May 1828. [NAS.E504.34.12]

ROBERT FULTON, master Hugh Graham, from Greenock *with
passengers* to New York on 10 October 1824. [DPCA#1145]

ROBERT KERR, Captain Boyd, from Greenock on 13 September
1825 bound for Quebec, arrived there on 21 October 1825.
[CCMA: 26.10.1825]

ROGER STEWART, from Greenock *with passengers* bound for
New York, arrived there on 9 June 1828, [NARA.M237.11];
from Greenock to Charleston, South Carolina, in November
1829. [NAS.E504.15.170]

ROLLO, Captain Thursby, from Leith on 4 August 1819, arrived in
Quebec on 28 September 1819; from Greenock to New
Providence in October 1829.
[MG.6.10.1819][NAS.E504.15.170]

ROMULUS, Captain Henderson, from Dumfries on 16 August
1822, arrived in Quebec on 17 October 1822.
[MG:23.10.1822]

ROSE OF GLASGOW, master James Fleming, from Port Glasgow
to St Kitts in January 1744; from Port Glasgow to Jamaica
and St Kitts in March 1745. [NAS.E504.28.1/2]

ROSE, a 400 ton brig, Captain Beveridge, arrived in Quebec on 19 May 1818 from Leith, [MG]; master David Johnston, from Leith bound for Quebec and Montreal in March 1822, arrived in Quebec on 11 June 1822 *with 45 passengers* from Leith. [EEC#17,266][MG:15.6.1822]; from Leith *with 45 passengers* to Quebec on 13 April 1823. [LCL.X.931]

ROSEMOUNT, from Arbroath, Angus, to St Johns, New Brunswick, on 26 March 1829. [NAS.E504.24.22]

ROSEOUS, Captain McLaren, from Greenock on 5 May 1823 *with 50 passengers* bound for Quebec, arrived there on 13 July 1823. [CC:19.7.1823] [QM:15.6.1823]

ROSINA, master A. Brown, arrived in Quebec on 5 June 1820 *with 1 passenger* from Greenock; arrived on 1 June 1819 from Greenock [QM:9.6.1819]

ROTHIEMURCHUS, 322 tons, master G. Watson, from Leith in March 1817 *with 105 passengers* bound for Quebec, arrived there on 1 June 1817; arrived in Quebec on 5 June 1818 *with 90 passengers* from Leith. [MG: 9.6.1817; 17.6.1818]

ROYAL CHARLOTTE, master W. C. Hobson, arrived in Quebec on 12 May 1819 *with 5 passengers* from Greenock; arrived in Quebec on 1 September 1824 *with 3 passengers* from Greenock.. [MG:19.5.1819][CC.8.9.1824]

ROYAL UNION, 260 tons, Captain D. Grant, from Leith to Quebec *with passengers* on 22 May 1822, arrived there on 11 August 1822. [EEC#17,300][MG:17.8.1822]

RUBY OF ABERDEEN, 80 tons, six guns, master Alexander Gordon, with a 9 man crew, from Aberdeen to Maryland on 23 April 1745. [NAS.E504.1.1]

RUBY, master John Udny, from Greenock *with passengers* bound for Halifax, Nova Scotia, and St John, New Brunswick, in February 1802. [GA#2]

RUPERT OF WHITEHAVEN, 130 tons, master Henry Braithwaite, arrived in Dumfries on 26 January 1761 from Virginia. [Dumfries Customs Records]

ST ANDREW OF GLASGOW, master John Brown, arrived in the Rappahannock River, Virginia, on 14 June 1739 from Glasgow; master Hugh Wallace, from Greenock on 12 March 1741 to Virginia. [VaGaz#152][CM#3273]

ST ANDREW, a 150 ton snow, master Arthur Gibbon, from Aberdeen *with passengers* bound for Kingston, Jamaica, in June 1758. [AJ#535/542]

ST DAVID OF DYSART, master William Jones, from Leith to Philadelphia by 1742. [NAS.AC9.1487]

ST DAVID OF IRVINE, master James MacFie, arrived in the Rappahannock River, Virginia, in June 1739 from Irvine; George Hutchison, from Irvine, Ayrshire, to Charleston, South Carolina, in July 1745. [VaGaz#152][NAS.E504.18.1]

ST HELENA, Captain Elliot, from Greenock on 7 April 1825 bound for Quebec, arrived there on 14 May 1825. [CCMA: 21.5.1825]

ST JOHNSTON OF PERTH, master Alexander Ross, arrived in Perth on 15 April 1764 from Philadelphia. [NAS.E504.27.5]

SALISBURY OF BOSTON, master Andrew Doberry, arrived in Port Glasgow on 21 August 1689 from Virginia; from Port Glasgow to Madeira in September 1689. [NAS.E72.19.14/15]

SALLY OF NORFOLK, master Robert Patterson, from Greenock to Jamaica in July 1746. [NAS.E504.15.2]

SALLY, 200 tons, master James Patrick, from Dundee to Grenada in 1773, and, via Leith, in March 1775. [AJ#1308][NAS.E504.11.9; E504.22.19]

SALLY, a brig, master W. Cumming, arrived in Quebec on 20 May 1818 *with 2 passengers* from Ayr; arrived in Quebec on 8 June 1820 *with passengers* from Greenock; arrived in Quebec on 26 June 1821 *with 16 passengers* from Glasgow; from Ayr on 11 April 1822 *with 12 passengers* bound for Quebec, arrived there on 5 June 1822. [MG: 27.6.1821; 12.6.1822]

SALMON OF CHESTER, master John Glover, arrived in Port Glasgow on 23 November 1681 from Nevis. [NAS.E72.19.5]

SALUTATION OF STRANRAER, 45 tons, master William Whiteside, from Hampton, Virginia, to Greenock, in September 1719. [NAS.GD180.457]

SAMUEL OF BELFAST, master John Russell, from Greenock to Barbados in January 1744. [NAS.E504.15.1]

SARAH, master Isaac Elwell, from Greenock bound for Charleston, South Carolina, in January 1802, sailed 6 March 1802; Captain Bowden, from the Clyde to New Orleans 23 August 1802. [GA#5/17, 67]

SARAH, a brig, Captain Dougall, from Greenock on 3 April 1825, arrived in Quebec on 12 May 1825. [CCMA: 11.5.1825]

SCEPTRE, a brig, from Leith on 12 April 1819 *with 1 passenger* bound for Quebec, arrived there on 17 May 1819, [MG:26.5.1819]; master Walter Smith, from Leith to New York in May 1822. [EEC#17,290]; Captain Smith, from Inverkeithing to New York in July 1822. [NAS.E504.16.1]

SCIENCE, from Greenock *with passengers* to New Orleans, arrived there on 13 December 1826. [NARA.M259/5]

SCIPIO OF GLASGOW, master John Lyon, arrived in Dundee on 23 December 1732 from Virginia; master John McCunn, arrived in Dundee on 23 February 1734 from Virginia; master John Clark, from the Clyde to Virginia in 1735; master John Clark from the Upper District of the James River, Virginia, to Glasgow on 19 August 1736. [GHG#210] [NAS.CE70.1.2] [VaGaz#7]

SCIPIO, master Robert Chisholm, from Greenock to St Kitts in December 1762; master Andrew Lyon, from Greenock via St Kitts to Maryland in February 1765; from Greenock to Nevis and St Kitts in January 1767. [NAS.E504.15.11/13/14]

SCOTIA, a brig, Captain Erskine, from Dundee to Jamaica in January 1822; from Dundee to Kingston, Jamaica, in September 1823, arrived there on 23 March 1824. [NAS.E504.11.23][DPCA#1103/1141]

SCOTIA, a brig, Captain W. Robinson, arrived in Quebec on 15 May 1820 from Aberdeen; from Aberdeen on 29 March 1824, arrived in Quebec on 30 May 1824; arrived in Quebec on 29 September 1824 from Aberdeen; from Aberdeen on 28 March 1825 bound for Quebec, arrived there on 11 May 1825; from Aberdeen on 29 July 1825 bound for Quebec, arrived there on 16 September 1825.[QM][CC.6.10.1824] [CCMA: 11.5.1825; 21.9.1825][MG:5.6.1824]

SCOTIA, Captain Simpson, arrived in Quebec during August 1829 *with 33 passengers* from Greenock. [QM: 4.8.1829]

SEAHORSE OF PHILADELPHIA, master Francis Blair, arrived in Campbeltown, Argyll, on 18 February 1757 from Philadelphia. [NAS.E504.8.2]

SEAFLOWER OF IRVINE, master William Hindman, from Irvine, Ayrshire, to Antigua in September 1714, [NAS.E508.8.6]

SEVEN STARS OF LONDON, master Arthur Moncreiff, from Port Glasgow to Montserrat on 17 November 1690. [NAS.E72.15.22]

SHAKESPEARE, Captain Goldie, from Aberdeen in May 1825, arrived in Quebec on 2 July 1825; from Dundee to Mobile and New Orleans in October 1829. [CCMA: 6.7.1825] [NAS.E504.11.26]

SHANNAN, master Archibald Orr, from Greenock to Barbados in November 1758. [NAS.E504.15.9]

SHARP, master James Bruce, arrived in Stranraer, Wigtownshire, on 11 May 1769 from Port North Potomac, Maryland. [NAS.E504.34.5]

SHAW, master Archibald Douglas, arrived in Port Glasgow on 5 December 1734 from Virginia; from the Clyde to Virginia in 1735. [NAS.E512/1455][GHG#210]

SIR EDWARD PELLEW, 307 tons, master W. Orr, from Greenock to New Providence in 1810. [L]

SIR JAMES KEMPT, from Dundee to New York in December 1828. [NAS.E504.11.26]

SIR J. H. CRAIG, master James Deas, arrived in Quebec on 7 May 1819 from Leith; arrived in Quebec on 15 July 1820 *with 100 passengers* from Leith. [MG:19.5.1819]

SIR WILLIAM WALLACE, a brig, Captain Anderson, from Aberdeen on 20 July 1824, arrived in Quebec on 8 September 1824; from Aberdeen on 26 March 1825 *with passengers* bound for Quebec, arrived there on 13 May 1825; from Aberdeen on 1 August 1825 bound for Quebec, arrived there on 16 September 1825; from Aberdeen to Miramichi, New Brunswick, in July 1827. [CC.15.9.1824] [CCMA:18.5.1825; 21.9.1825] [NAS.E504.1.32]

SIREN OF GLASGOW, master John Harrison, from St Kitts to the River Clyde in 1686. [NAS.AC7.8]

SISTERS, a brig, master James Dobie, from Dysart, Fife, to Philadelphia on 12 February 1822. [EEC#17,252]

SKENE, a brig, Captain Bishop, arrived in Quebec on 18 May 1820 *with 22 passengers* from Leith. [QM]

SOCIETY OF GLASGOW, master John Loving, arrived in Port Glasgow on 13 September 1696 from Virginia. [NAS.E72.15.23]

SOCIETY OF WORKINGTON, master John Thomson, from Greenock to Antigua in December 1716, [NAS.E508.10.6]

SOMERSETSHIRE, Captain Ross, from Inverkeithing to Jamaica in January 1825; from Inverkeithing to Jamaica in October 1825. [NAS.E504.16.1]

SOPHIA, master Samuel Bowman, from the Clyde to Virginia in 1735; master Samuel Bowman, from the Upper District of the James River, Virginia, to Glasgow on 13 September 1736. [GHG#210][VaGaz#7]

SOPHIA OF GREENOCK, a brig, master A. Moore, arrived in Quebec on 17 May 1818 from Greenock; arrived in Quebec on 8 September 1818 *with 160 passengers* from Greenock; Captain Neil, from Greenock on 3 April 1825 *with passengers* bound for Quebec, arrived there on 13 May 1825; from Glasgow on 26 March 1826 *with 15 passengers* bound for Quebec, arrived there on 3 May 1825; arrived in Quebec in October 1826 *with 43 passengers* from Greenock. [MG] [CCMA:18.5.1825; 10.5.1826][QM: 7.10.1826]

SOVEREIGN, master A. Pearson, arrived in Quebec on 3 June 1820 *with 49 passengers* from Leith. [QM]

SPECULATION, Captain Allan, arrived in Quebec on 12 September 1819 *with 87 passengers* from Oban; Captain Douglas, arrived in Quebec on 30 June 1820 *with 120 passengers* from Greenock. [MG.22.9.1819]

SPEEDWELL OF GALWAY, arrived in Glasgow on 8 September 1670 from Virginia. [NAS.E72.10.2]

SPEEDWELL OF BOSTON, arrived in Inverness from America in May 1711. [SC: 26.5.1711]

SPEEDWELL, master James Colhoun, from the Clyde to Jamaica in 1735. [GHG#210]

SPENCER OF GLASGOW, master James Scott, arrived in Greenock on 22 November 1742 from Virginia. [NAS.E504.15.1]

SPENCER, from Greenock on 24 July 1823 *with 23 passengers* bound for Quebec, arrived there on 24 September 1823. [CC:1.10.1823]

SPIERS, master John Lamont, from Port Glasgow to Barbados in October 1775 and in March 1777, [NAS.E504.28.25/27]

SPOONER, master Daniel Graham, from Greenock to St Kitts in October 1767. [NAS.E504.15.14]

SPRIGHTLY, from Dundee to Quebec in August 1829. [NAS.E504.11.26]

SQUIRREL, from Scotland to St Kitts in 1722. [NAS.AC9/1022]

STANDARD, from Dundee to New York in November 1828 and in November 1829. [NAS.E504.11.26]

STAPLETON, a brig, Captain Amory, arrived in Quebec on 18 June 1818 from Greenock. [MG:24.6.1818]

STAR OF PETERHEAD, master Thomas Sprittiman, from Leith to Virginia in November 1667. [NAS.RD3.16.256]

STAR, master John Matthewson, arrived in Quebec on 11 September 1819 from Aberdeen. [MG.22.9.1819]

SUCCESS OF CHESTER, master Joshua Glover, at Nantasket Roads, New England, in June 1686, bound for Virginia, probably from Scotland. [CW:MS46.02]

SUCCESS, a brig, master John Graham, arrived in the Upper District of the James River, Virginia, on 18 September 1745 from Dumfries. [VaGaz#480]

SUCCESS OF DUNDEE, master Patrick Ogilvie, from Dundee to Antigua in October 1763. [NAS.E504.11.5]

SUFFOLK, Captain Thean, from Aberdeen on 1 April 1819, arrived in Quebec on 7 May 1819. [MG:19.5.1819]

SUPERIOR, master J. Birnie, arrived in Quebec on 5 June 1820 *with 4 passengers* from Montrose; arrived in Quebec on 15 May 1821 *with 6 passengers* from Montrose. [QM][MG: 23.5.1821; 8.6.1822]

SUSANNA OF SALTCOATS [later OF IRVINE], master William Galt, from Greenock in March 1741 to Virginia; arrived in Greenock on 28 November 1741 from Virginia; from Greenock to Virginia on 17 April 1742; master John

Heasty, arrived in Greenock on 14 December 1742 from Virginia.
[CM#3273/3313/3372][EEC#5399][NAS,E504.15.1]

SUSANNA, an American ship, master Thomas Bennet, from Greenock to Charleston, South Carolina, in May 1802, sailed 11 June 1802. [GA#1/37/46]

SUSANNAH, master Robert Ewing, from Greenock to Antigua in October 1758. [NAS.E504.15.9]

SUSIE, master Cuthbert Kelburn, from Greenock via Cork to St Kitts and Antigua in January 1763; from Greenock to St Kitts in November 1763. [NAS.E504.15.11/12]

SWALLOW OF INVERNESS, master David Nevoy, from Inverness to Jamaica in October 1728. [NAS.E508.22.6/69]

SWALLOW OF DUNDEE, 75 tons, master William Hill, from Leith to Grenada in November 1770, November 1772, and in November 1773. [NAS.E504.22.16/17/18]

SWALLOW, arrived in New Brunswick in 1822 from Glencaple and Dumfries, Dumfries-shire. [DWJ.22.11.1822]

SWAN OF DUNBARTON, arrived in Glasgow on 27 August 1666 from Virginia. [NAS.E72.10.1]

SWAN OF DONAGHADEE, master Andrew Gregg, arrived in Ayr by August 1690 from Virginia. [AA.B6.18.4/373]

SWAN, a brigantine, master J. Hatrick, from Greenock to Trinidad in January 1802, also in June 1802. [GA#1/2/50]

SWEEPSTAKE, Captain White, from Kirkcudbright to America around 1626. [DBR]

SWIFT OF GREENOCK, Captain Smith, was captured on the Banks of Newfoundland by a French frigate in December 1793 and taken to Brest, France. [AJ#2399]

SWINGER, a brig, master Alexander McFarlane, from Greenock to Trinidad in April 1802. [GA#1/26]

SYLVIA OF LIVERPOOL, from Inverness to Jamaica on 4 October 1758. [NAS.E508.26.6]

TAMARLANE OF GREENOCK, Captain McKillop, from Greenock on 21 July 1825 *with 30 passengers* bound for Quebec, arrived there on 26 August 1825. [QM: 24.8.1825][CCMA: 31.8.1825]

TARBOLTON, Captain Boyd, from Greenock on 18 April 1825 bound for Quebec, arrived there on 19 May 1825; from Irvine, Ayrshire, to Dalhousie, New Brunswick, in April 1829. [CCMA: 25.5.1825][NAS.E504.18.20]

THANE OF FIFE, master William Wemyss, from Leith to South Carolina on 10 June 1742. [CM#3394]

THETIS OF GLASGOW, master William Andrews, arrived in Montrose, Angus, from the James River, Virginia, on 28 September 1749; arrived in Montrose on 20 August 1750 from the James River, Virginia; from Montrose to Barbados 8 September 1750. [NAS.E504.24.2]

THISTLE OF PORT GLASGOW, 160 tons, master John Wilson, arrived in Hampton, Virginia, on 13 November 1738 via Philadelphia. [VSS#99]

THISTLE OF GLASGOW, master Colin Dunlop, arrived in Port Glasgow on 3 December 1735 from Virginia; from the Upper District of the James River, Virginia, to Glasgow on 13 May 1737; master John Orr, from Greenock on 17 February 1741 to Virginia; arrived in Greenock on 28 November 1741 from Virginia; from Greenock to Virginia on 20 February 1742; arrived in Greenock on 19 November 1742 from Virginia. [CM#3262/3313/3350][NAS.E512/1455; E504.15.1] [VaGaz#43]

THISTLE OF IRVINE, later OF SALTCOATS, a brig, master Robert Brown, arrived in Greenock on 23 June 1741 from Virginia; from Greenock to Virginia on 1 May 1742; arrived in Port Glasgow on 23 March 1743 from Maryland; arrived at Hampton, Virginia, on 3 September 1745 from Glasgow. [CM#3317/3378][NAS.E504.28.1][VaGaz#480]

THISTLE OF LEITH, 150 tons, master John Murray, from Leith to Virginia in April 1753, and in March 1754, also in December 1754, June 1755, and January 1757. [NAS.E504.22.5/6/7]

THISTLE, master Robert Baird, from Greenock to St Kitts and Martinique in January 1763. [NAS.E504.15.11]

THISTLE OF GLASGOW, 160 tons, master Colin Dunlop, from the Clyde to Virginia in 1735, arrived in Port Glasgow in December 1735 from Virginia; master John Wilson,arrived in Hampton, Virginia, on 13 November 1738 from Philadelphia. [GHG#210][NAS.E512/1455][NA.CO5/1320.R3]

THISTLE, a snow, master Alexander Marquis, from Greenock to New York in September 1770. [CM#7563]

THISTLE OF ABERDEEN, master R. Allan, arrived in Quebec during October 1821 *with 43 passengers* from Tobermory, Mull, Argyll; from Tobermory on 8 July 1822 *with 56 passengers* bound for Quebec, arrived there on 19 September 1822. [QM:19.10.1821][MG:25.9.1822]

THOMAS OF GREENOCK, master William Watt, from Greenock to Virginia on 24 July 1740; arrived in Greenock on 27 June 1741 from Virginia; from Greenock to Carolina on 15 August 1741; arrived in Greenock on 17 April 1742 from South Carolina; Captain Gregory, from Greenock to North Carolina on 10 June 1742. [CM#3172/3318/3338/3372/3394]

THOMAS OF GLASGOW, master Matthew Murchie later George Buchanan, arrived in Greenock on 8 August 1740 from Virginia. [CM#3180]

THOMAS, master ....Robertson, arrived in the James River, Virginia, in March 1772 from Glasgow. [VG:12.3.1772]

THOMAS, Captain Macy, from Greenock to New York in April 1802. [GA#1/26]

THOMAS, a bark, Captain Rodgers, from Leith on 1 August 1825 bound for Quebec, arrived there on 16 September 1825. [CCMA: 21.9.1825]

THOMAS AND BETTY OF MONTROSE, master Robert Mudie, arrived in Montrose in March 1749 from Virginia; from Montrose, Angus, to Virginia 11 November 1749; master Robert Beattie, from Montrose to Virginia 23 April 1750. [NAS.CE53.1.4; E504.24.2]

THOMAS AND FRANCES OF BOSTON, master Nathaniel Hammond, from St Kitts to Leith in 1707. [NAS.AC10.60]

THOMAS AND JOHN OF PORT GLASGOW, Captain Berry, from Greenock on 4 April 1741 to Barbados. [CM#3282]

THOMAS LAURIE, a brig, Captain McCall, from Greenock *with 13 passengers* bound for Quebec on 20 July 1825, arrived there on 4 September 1825. [CCMA:10.9.1825]

THOMAS MARTIN, a brig, Captain Edwards, from Greenock in April 1817, arrived in Quebec on 3 June 1817. [MG:9.6.1817]

THOMAS PEEL, a brig, Captain Elliot, from Greenock on 2 September 1825 bound for Quebec, arrived there on 10 October 1825. [CCMA:15.10.1825]

THOMPSON'S PACKET OF DUMFRIES, Captain Lookup, arrived in Quebec on 6 July 1822 *with 40 passengers* from Dumfries on 23 April 1822. [QM: 9.7.1822][MG:13.7.1822]; Captain Whitehead, from Wigtown on 25 July 1825 bound for Quebec, arrived there on 16 September 1825; from Dumfries to St John, New Brunswick, on 31 March 1829; from Dumfries to Richibucto, New Brunswick, on 4 September 1829.[QM:9.7.1822] [CCMA:21.9.1825] [NAS.E504.9.10]

THORNTONS, Captain Holmes, arrived in Quebec on 7 September 1819 *with 24 passengers* from Glasgow; from Greenock *with passengers* to New Orleans, arrived there on 20 November 1821. [MG:15.9.1819][NARA.M259/2]

THREE CHRISTIANS OF GLASGOW, master John Esdale, from Greenock to Barbados in November 1716; master Hugh Hill, from Greenock to Barbados in November 1717. [NAS.E508.10.6; E508.12.6]

THREE SISTERS, master David Lang, from Greenock to Nevis in November 1758. [NAS.E504.15.9]

TIBBIE, master Cuthbert Kelburn, from Greenock to St Kitts and Montserrat in April 1767. [NAS.E504.15.14]

TOBACCO PLANTATION, Captain Biskey, from Inverkeithing to Boston in August 1824. [NAS.E504.16.1]

TODS, a brig, Captain McPherson, arrived in Quebec on 22 July 1817 *with 42 passengers* from Dundee. [MG]

TRAFALGAR, 300 ton brig, Captain Mitchell, arrived in Quebec on 31 July 1817 *with 100 passengers* from Leith, [MG]; master James Henderson, from Bo'ness to New York *with passengers* in May 1822, [EEC#17,278]; from Leith *with 11 passengers* to New York on 17 April 1823. [LCL.X.932]

TRAVELLER, Captain Goldie, arrived in Quebec on 11 September 1819 *with 142 passengers* from Aberdeen; arrived in Quebec on 16 May 1820 *with 20 passengers* from Aberdeen. [MG.22.9.1819][QM]

TRIAL OF SALTCOATS, master Hugh Brown, from Greenock *with passengers* to Virginia on 20 August 1739, arrived in Hampton, Virginia, during October 1739; arrived in Greenock on 21 November 1741 from Virginia; from Greenock to Virginia on 20 February 1742. [VG:2.11.1739][CM#3020/3309/3350]

TRIAL OF ABERDEEN, master Charles Stuart, from Philadelphia in November 1739 bound for Aberdeen. [ACA.APB.3.87]

TRIM, a brig, Captain Lyon, from Glasgow on 2 April 1818, arrived in Quebec on 2 June 1818. [MG:10.6.1818]

TRITON, master Walter Stirling, from the Clyde to Barbados in 1735. [GHG#210]

TRITON OF LONDON, later OF GLASGOW, master John Boyd, arrived in Greenock on 12 December 1741 from Jamaica; from Greenock to Virginia on 27 February 1742; arrived in Port Glasgow on 15 March 1743 from Virginia;

master John McCunn, from Port Glasgow to the Isle of May, (Isle of Maia, Cape Verde Islands) in December 1744. [CM#3318/3351][NAS.E504.28.1/2]

TROPIC, Captain Anderson, from Inverkeithing to Jamaica in February 1826. [NAS.E504.16.1]

TRUE BLUE OF ANSTRUTHER, 70 tons, master Alexander Boytar, from Leith to Grenada on 21 September 1769, to Tobago and Grenada in December 1770, and to Grenada in October 1771. [NAS.E504.22.15/16/17]

TRUE BRITON, a brig, master James Reid, arrived in Quebec on 5 June 1820 *with 54 passengers* from Greenock; arrived in Quebec on 1 June 1821 *with 10 passengers* from Greenock; arrived in Quebec during June 1822 *with 45 passengers* from Leith; Captain Reid, from Greenock on 11 April 1825 *with passengers* bound for Quebec, arrived there on 18 May 1825; from Irvine *with 10 passengers* on 29 April 1826 bound for Quebec, arrived there on 13 June 1826. [MG:6.6.1821] [QM:11.6.1822][CCMA: 25.5.1825; 21.6.1826]

TRUSTY, a bark, Captain Mather, from Greenock on 19 April 1825 bound for Quebec, arrived there on 26 May 1825. [CCMA:1.6.1825]

TWO BROTHERS OF BOSTON, a brigantine, master Robert Gass, arrived in Port Glasgow on 1 May 1690 from Virginia. [NAS.E72.19.18]

TWO BROTHERS OF FRASERBURGH, BB, 50 tons, master George Elmslie, from Aberdeen to Antigua in February 1751. [NAS.E504.1.3]

TWO BROTHERS, Captain Blues, from Aberdeen to Newfoundland on 13 May 1774. [AJ#1375]

TWO FRIENDS OF ST KITTS, an 80 ton ship, master John Ireland, from Dundee to North Carolina in June 1764. [NAS.E504.11.5]

TYGER, master James Birrell, from Burntisland to Grenada in October 1770, *'a blacksmith, well skilled in shoeing horses,* *will find good encouragement*'; master Charles Patton, from Leith to Grenada in November 1771. [CM#7570][NAS.E504.22.17]

UGIE, master J.Taylor, arrived in Quebec on 27 May 1820 from Peterhead. [QM]

UNICORN, master James Chalmers, from Ayr to St Kitts in 1663. [AA.B6.35.1]; from Ayr to the West Indies in 1665. [AA.B6.18.1]

UNION OF GLASGOW, master William Anderson, from Glasgow to Virginia on 16 November 1686. [NAS.E72.19.12]

UNION, master D. Ferguson, from Greenock to Savannah, Georgia, in February 1802, sailed on 16 February 1802. [GA#5/13]

UNION, a brig, master J. Ord, arrived in Quebec on 16 June 1818 *with 7 passengers* from Aberdeen. [MG:24.6.1818]

UNION, arrived in Quebec on 16 May 1820 from Greenock; master John Craig, arrived in Quebec on 11 October 1820 from Irvine; master M. Henry, arrived in Quebec on 16 May 1821 from Greenock. [MG.23.5.1821]

UNION, from Glasgow to Montreal in July 1829. [NAS.E504.13.57]

UNION GALLEY OF LEITH, master William Rogers, from Leith to Barbados in February 1709, [NAS.E508.4.6]

UNITY OF AYR, from Ayr to the West Indies in 1671, [AA.B6.24.3]; arrived in Ayr in September 1672 from Barbados, [AA.B6.18.4]; from Ayr to Barbados and Montserrat 10 March 1673, returned to Ayr from Barbados on 2 September 1673; from Ayr to the West Indies in 1674 but captured by the Dutch and taken to Amsterdam. [AA.B6.24.3]

UNITY OF DUMFRIES, 60 tons, master James Corbett, arrived in Hampton, Virginia, on 16 May 1738 via St Kitts. [NA.CO5/1320.R3][VSS#97]

UNITY OF GREENOCK, master William Service, arrived in Quebec during September 1792 *with passengers* from Greenock. [QGaz: 27.9.1792]

UNITY, Captain Morrison, from Greenock to Quebec in July 1802. [GA#1/46]

UNIVERSE, Captain Craigie, from Aberdeen to Cape Breton in April 1826, [NAS.E504.1.32]

URANIA, master W. Newton, arrived in Quebec on 19 May 1820 *with 20 passengers* from Leith; arrived in Quebec on 21 May 1821 from Leith; from Dundee to New Orleans and Mobile in November 1828.[QM][MG.23.5.1821] [NAS.E504.11.26]

VENUS, Captain Anderson, arrived in Quebec on 15 May 1821 *with 10 passengers* from Aberdeen; arrived in Quebec on 16 September 1821 from Aberdeen. [MG: 23.5.1821; 26.9.1821]

VERNON OF GLASGOW, master John Brown, arrived in Greenock on 23 November 1742 from Virginia; master Andrew Turner, from Greenock to Antigua in August 1743. [NAS.E504.15.1]

VIGILANT, a brig, Captain Hogg, from Leith on 8 April 1826 bound for Quebec, arrived there on 20 May 1826. [CCMA:27.5.1826]

VINE OF FALMOUTH, master William Hall, arrived in Port Glasgow on 15 May 1691 from Virginia. [NAS.E72.15.21]

VIRGINIA, master Alexander Thomson, arrived in the James River, Virginia, on 24 May 1760 from Glasgow; master Alexander Thomson, arrived in the James River, Virginia, on 24 May 1766 from Glasgow via Rotterdam. [VG:30.5.1760; 30.5.1766]

WAKEFIELD, master Robert Carter, from Glasgow on 2 August 1819 *with 20 passengers* bound for Quebec, arrived there on 25 September 1819. [MG.6.10.1819]

WALLACE, master Hugh Moody, from Greenock to Jamaica in August 1765, in September 1766, and in August 1767. [NAS.E504.15.13/14]

WARNER, a brig, Captain Stephenson, from Greenock on 5 May 1824 bound for Quebec, arrived there on 26 June 1824; from Greenock on 11 May 1825 *with 14 passengers* bound for Quebec, arrived there on 21 June 1825; Captain Crawford, from Greenock *with 13 passengers* bound for Quebec, arrived there on 30 June 1826; arrived in Quebec during July 1827 *with 43 passengers* from Greenock; from Irvine, Ayrshire, to Dalhousie, New Brunswick, in July 1828; from Irvine to Dalhousie in January 1829; from Irvine to Dalhousie in April 1829. [CC.3.7.1824] [CCMA: 29.6.1825; 5.7.1826] [QM:24.7.1827][NAS.E504.18.20]

WASHINGTON, Captain Noyes, from Port Glasgow to New York in June 1802. [GA#1/42]

WATERLOO, master J. Kendal, arrived in Quebec on 9 September 1818 *with 108 passengers* from Fort William, Inverness-shire. [QM: 10.9.1818][MG]

WELCOME OF GREENOCK, master Robert Rea, from Greenock to Barbados in March 1718. [NAS.E508.12.6]

WELCOME OF GREENOCK, master John Boyd, from Greenock to Antigua on 27 December 1740; arrived in Greenock on 22 August 1741 from Antigua. [CM#3240/3344]; master Thomas Watson, from Port Glasgow to Antigua in December 1742. [NAS.E504.15.1]

WELCOME OF BRISTOL, master Thomas Chadsey, arrived in Campbeltown, Argyll, on 4 June 1744 from Virginia. [NAS.E504.8.1]

WELCOME OF CAMPBELTOWN, master Alexander Leith, arrived in Campbeltown, Argyll, from South Carolina and Lisbon, on 31 January 1751. [NAS.E504.8.2]

WELCOME, Captain McColl, arrived in Quebec during October 1826 *with 15 passengers* from Greenock. [QM:10.10.1826]

WESTMORELAND, from Dundee to New York in July 1829. [NAS.E504.11.26]

WHARTON OF WHITEHAVEN, from Glasgow (?) to Virginia in 1725; master James Wharrey, from Virginia to Glasgow, 1724-1725; master James Wharrey, from Glasgow to Virginia, 1734. [NAS.AC10.88; AC9.1116; AC7.35.58; AC8.498]

WILLIAM OF GLASGOW, master William Eccles, from Port Glasgow to Barbados in September 1713; master John Alexander, from Greenock to Barbados in September 1714, [NAS.E508.7.6; E508.8.6]

WILLIAM OF DONAGHADEE, Captain Davison, from Loch Bracadale, Skye, and Harris, *with passengers* bound for Philadelphia in October 1739, voyage abandoned at Donaghadee. [NA.SP63.402]

WILLIAM AND FRANCES OF BOSTON, master Francis Ellis, arrived in Glasgow on 8 August 1686 from Virginia; from Glasgow via Belfast to New England on 13 September 1686. [NAS.E72.19.12]

WILLIAM AND HENRY, from Inverkeithing to Jamaica in January 1827. [NAS.E504.16.1]

WILLIAM AND JAMES OF GLASGOW, master Richard Barringstone, from Greenock to Barbados in September 1714, [NAS.E508.8.6]

WILLIAM AND JEAN OF GLASGOW, to New England in 1678. [NAS.AC7.4]

WILLIAM AND JOHN OF GLASGOW, master William Dick, arrived in Montrose, Angus, on 6 December 1732 from Virginia. [NAS.CE53.1.2]

WILLIAM AND JOHN OF IRVINE, master James Thomson, from Greenock to Virginia on 25 July 1741, [CM#3332]; from Irvine, Ayrshire, to Virginia in July 1743. [NAS.E501.18.1]

WILLIAM AND MARGARET, master Jonathan Reynolds, from Greenock to New York in March 1802. [GA#6]

WILLIAM AND MARY OF LONDON, master William Hall, from Port Glasgow to Nevis on 12 September 1691. [NAS.E72.15.22]

WILLIAM AND SARAH OF BARBADOS, master John Smith, arrived in Port Glasgow via Belfast on 24 September 1691. [NAS.E72.19.22]

WILLIAM AND SARAH OF ABERDEEN, (BB), master Patrick Beattie, from Montrose, Angus, to Virginia 20 June 1750. [NAS.E504.24.2]

WILLIAM MINOR, master William Wilson, arrived in Quebec on 15 July 1819 *with 96 passengers* from Aberdeen. [MG:21.7.1819]

WILLIAMS, Captain Bowman, from Leith on 20 May 1825 *with 4 passengers* bound for Quebec, arrived there on 15 July 1825. [CCMA:20.7.1825]

WILMINGTON OF CAPE FEAR, 100 tons, master Thomas Murray, from Leith to Jamaica in October 1754, in November 1755, in January 1757, and in June 1758. [NAS.E504.22.6/7/8]

WOLF, master William Marshall, from Port Glasgow to Jamaica in February 1777. [NAS.E504.28.27]

YORK, master Andrew McVey, from Port Glasgow to Barbados in January 1777. [NAS.E504.28.27]

YOUNG NORVAL, Captain Luck, arrived in Quebec on 26 May 1820 *with 37 passengers* from Greenock. [QM: 26.5.1820]

YTHAN, Captain Cairns, arrived in Quebec during September 1826 *with 20 passengers* from Greenock. [QM:12.9.1826]

ZOON VAN AMSTERDAM, master Adrian Scott, from Holland to the West Indies then Virginia and finally to Leith in 1708. [NAS.AC10.72]

........., master John Gourlay, arrived in Leith on 10 March 1667 from Virginia. [NAS.E72.15.7]

.........., Captain Young, from Burntisland to Virginia in 1716. [NAS.AC8.199]

.........., Captain Thomas Baillie, from Inverness to Virginia in 1728. [NAS.AC10.132]

.... master Andrew Geils, arrived in the James River, Virginia, during June 1737 from Glasgow. [VaGaz#48]

.........., Captain Orr, arrived in Boston during June 1770 from Greenock. [BoNL#3478]

ADDENDUM

Ships via Africa

AFRICA, 90 tons, master William Seaton, from Greenock in September 1763 bound for Africa, left Grenada on 24 November 1764 for Glasgow; master James Noble, from Greenock in July 1765 bound for Africa. [NAS.E504.15.11/12/13; NA.CO.106/1]

AGNES OF BOSTON, 110 tons, master Robert Duthie, arrived in the Upper James River, Virginia, on 15 September 1758 via Bance Island; from Greenock in March 1759 bound for Africa, returned to the Clyde via Virginia in February 1760; from Greenock in March 1760 bound for Bance Island, Sierra Leone, arrived in Virginia in September 1760, returned to Greenock on 21 May 1761; from Greenock in January 1762 bound for the Gambia River, arrived in the Upper James River, Virginia, on 7 October 1762, returned to Greenock in March 1763. [VSS#159][NAS.E504.15.9/10/11]

CAROLINA, master John Kennedy, from Glasgow to Guinea and Maryland by 1770. [NAS.AC7.53]

COATS, 120 tons, master Ambrose Green, from Greenock in May 1766 bound for Africs; returned to Greenock in September 1765 from Africa and Barbados. [NAS.E504.15.13]

DELIGHT OF MONTROSE, master C. J. Elphinstone, from Montrose via Holland to the Gambia, returned to Leith from Virginia and Gambia in March 1754. [NAS.E504.22.5/6; NA.CO388/45, dd.162-7]

FRIENDSHIP OF AYR, master John Aitken, from Ayr via Africa to the West Indies in 1744. [NAS.AC8.653]

FRIENDSHIP OF GLASGOW, master John Shannon, from Port Glasgow bound for the Isle of May, Cape Verde Islands, in March 1747. [NAS.E504.28.3]

GEORGE GALLEY, master David Buckland, from Glasgow in 1717 bound for Africa, Barbados, and Virginia; arrived in Virginia from Barbados, 1717. [NA.T70/6; CO5.1320/R3]

GLASGOW OF LEITH, 70 tons, master George C. Smith, from Leith on 22 May 1764 bound for the Gambia. [NAS.E504.22.11]

GRAEMIE OF GLASGOW, master George Hunter, from Port Glasgow via the Isle of May, Cape Verde Islands, to Virginia, in February 1749. [NAS.E504.28.4]

HANNOVER, 60 tons, master Garrett Garretts, from Glasgow in 1720 bound for the Ivory and the Gold Coasts, also Old Calabar, then to Barbados and the Leeward Islands. [NAS.AC9/1042; AC7/33/433-583]

ISABEL OF GREENOCK, master John Park, arrived in Virginia from Barbados in 1710s. [NA.CO5.1320.R3]

JUBA, master Stephen Rowan, from Greenock in July 1765 bound for Africa and Barbados, returned to Greenock in July 1767. [NAS.E504.15.12/14]

LOYALTY, 80 tons, master (1) Mungo Graham, (2) Patrick Cheape, from Glasgow in 1718 bound for West Africa and Barbados., arrived in Barbados in December 1719. [NA.CO33/15][NAS.AC9/769; AC16/1/316-400]

MARIA, master George Forrester, from Greenock in September 1763 bound for Africa. [NAS.E504.15.11]

MAXWELL, 150 tons, master William Seaton, from Greenock in October 1761 bound for Africa. [NAS.E504.15.10]

METHVEN OF GLASGOW, 100 tons, masters Duncan Campbell, Robert Ramsay, and John Coppell, from Port Glasgow and Greenock in April 1751 via Rotterdam bound for the Gold Coast, later recorded at the Windward Coast of Guinea, before sailing for St Kitts. [NAS.E504.28.5; E504.15.5][Aberdeen Journal#236]

NEPTUNE, master James Lyon, from Glasgow in 1730 bound for Africa then Barbados, from Barbados in July 1731 bound for Glasgow. [NA.CO.33/16]

OTHELLO, 110 tons, master John Cousins, from Greenock in September 1763 bound for Africa, from there to Jamaica, stranded on the coast of Donegal, Ireland, on return voyage on 6 December 1764. [NAS.E504.15.11/13]

PATRIOT PITT, master John Cousins, from Greenock in September 1761 bound for the Gold Coast, returned to Greenock from Africa and Martinique in May 1763. [NAS.E504.15.10/11; CS95/506]

PEGGY OF GLASGOW, master William Walkinshaw, from Port Glasgow bound for the Isle of May, Cape Verde Islands, in 1747. [NAS.E504.28.3]

POTOMAC MERCHANT OF MONTROSE, masters (1) Thomas Gibson, (2) Richard Hartley, from Montrose, Angus, via Rotterdam to Bonny and Virginia in 1751, returned to Montrose in December 1752. [NAS.E504.24.2/3]

ST GEORGE OF MONTROSE, 100 tons, master Richard Hartley, from Montrose, Angus, via Veere, Zealand, to Africa and Antigua in March 1753, returned to Montrose in June 1754. [NAS.E504.24.3; AC7.46.51-62]

SPENCER, master David Skinner, from Port Glasgow to the Isle of May, Cape Verde Islands, in December 1748. [NAS.E504.28.4]

SUCCESS OF MONTROSE, 75 tons, master James Renny, from Montrose, Angus, to Africa and the West Indies in 1735.

TWO BROTHERS OF LEITH, master Robert Richardson (?), from Leith to Guinea and the West Indies, returning via Holland in 1706. [NAS.CC8.8.83/25]

1729   36,68

1730   53,64,109,

1731   12,31,68,

1732   67,83,91,105,

1734   4, 44,64,67,71,91,93,105,

1735   3,4,5,8,10,12,19,21,26,34,39,43,48,
53,58,61,65,67,75,76,82,83,86,87,91,93,94,
97,98,100,110,

1736   6,19,36,47,67,91,94,

1737   40,42,43,97,107,

1738   3,16,42,68,71,97,98,102,

1739   3,4,5,12,27,40,49,50,57,63,71,73,
74,90,100,105,

1740   4,5,8,12,23,27,31,37,42,49,50,
52,64,68,71,72,73,75,98,104,

1741   2,5,6,9,10,12,13,19,21,26,27,29,
30,31,36,37,39,40,42,42,49,50,53,55,58,
61,63,64,67,68,70,71,72,73,74,76,79,
80,81,83,86,87,89,95,97,98,99,100,104,
105,

1742   5,6,9,10,12,13,15,21,27,36,37,
40,50,53,55,58,59,61,63,64,67,68,71,
74,76,80,83,90,94,95,96,97,98,100,103,
104,

1743   5,6,8,15,24,27,30,42,58,59,63,
67,71,74,97,100,105,

1744   27,31,37,42,59,71,74,88,91,101,

104,108,

1745   6,7,8,13,27,30,31,37,51,55,57,
60,71,74,82,88,89,90,95,97,

1746   1,2,13,27,30,31,48,59,72,82,83,90,

1747   15,16,24,27,40,57,82,108,109,

1748   5,8,11,17,19,20,31,40,41,50,
60,63,110,

1749   2,13,17,26,29,42,70,97,99,108,

1750   4,6,13,26,27,29,51,54,67,82,97,
99,105,

1751   8,19,54,61,78,82,101,104,109,

1752   19,26,27,49,60,

1753   4,8,19,27,32,49,61,72,75,98,109,

1754   2,12,32,35,49,72,82,85,98,105,108,

1755   2,58,81,98,105,

1756   21,58,80,

1757   59,64.92,98,105,

1758   12,20,35,42,59,60,62,67,80,90,
92,96,97,100,105,107,

1759   42,107,

1760   11,14,47,55,80,103,107,

1761   58,90,109,

1762   12,15,19,22,40,48,55,72,76,80,
91,107,

1763   6,11,12,13,15,43,44,45,47,49,
54,55,63,74,80,95,96,98,107,109,

1764   1,8,12,19,45,46,49,51,54,62,68,

80,90,101,107,108,

1765 34,48,49,55,59,75,91,107,

1766 6,8,11,15,19,28,46,47,48,55,75,

76,103,104,108,

1767 8,9,11,12,15,21,26,38,43,44,47,

55,62,63,72,75,76,91,94,100,104,108,

1768 3,10,11,26,31,38,42,44,47,55.

56,64,69

1769 13,14,18,24,38,46,53,92,101,

1770 9,18,23,24,28,29,37,39,40,46,53,

57,61,62,63,69,79,80,96,98,101,107,

1771 4,18,21,23,35,37,41,63,69,76,80,

101,102,

1772 2,4,7,11,15,18,21,24,35,37,53,

69,76,78,80,81,84,96,98,

1773 5,8,11,18,21,38,46,50,53,69,75,

79,90,96,

1774 2,8,18,50,75,84,101,

1775 11,31,34,38,40,46,53,73,75,90,94,

1776 11,12,28,36,48,55,57,64,75,87,

1777 3,6,22,30,34,43,46,53,55,59,62,80,

94,**106,**

1779 18,39,

1782 12

1785 80,85,

1786 84

1787 32,

1788 56,71,

1790 15,

1792 103,

1793 24,96,

1794 51,

1796 70,

1801 36,

1802 1,2,3,4,5,6,7,9,10,14,15,16,17,18,

20,21,22,23,24,26,27,28,30,33,34,35,36,39

44,46,48,49,51,53,54,55,56,58,60,62,63,

65,66,69,70,72,73,74,75,76,77,78,79,80,83,

86,89,91,96,98,102,103,104,106,

1804 22,

1805 54,86,

1806 47,

1808 50,

1809 3,14,70,

1810 4,28,40,93,

1811 18,

1812 49,

1814 14,105,

1815 35,65,

1816 16,49,82,

1817 4,5,8,9,16,20,34,38,45,47,50,51,

56,57,58,60,62,63,69,74,76,77,78,79,81,

82,83,84,85,86,87,89,99,100,

1818 2,7,10,13,16,20,22,24,29,34,35,36,

38,41,42,46,49,50,51,56,69,74,77,78,79,82,

85,86,87,89,90,94,95,100,102,104,

1819 7,10,16,17,18,20,29,30,33,34,39,41,

43,47,51,54,56,57,60,65,66,69,76,77,78,79,

81,82,83,84,85,86,87,88,91,93,94,95,99,100,

103,105,

1820 4,8,11,14,15,20,21,22,24,26,27,29,

33,36,41, 43,47,51,52,56,64,65,67,70,73,

78,79,81,83,84,85,86,87,88,89,90,92,93,94,

95,100,101,102,103,106,

1821 11,16,17,20,22,28,29,30,39,43,45,54,

58,59,65,69,70,77,79,80,81,85,86,88,90,95,

98,99,101,102,103,

1822 2,7,9,16,20,22,24,26,28,29,30,32,39,44,

46,54,56,58,64,65,67,70,73,74,77,78,81,84,85

86,88,89,91,92,93,96,98,99,100,101,

1823, 3,4,7,11,14,15,16,20,22,26,28,29,

30,32,36,43,44,45,52,56,57,58,59,60,62,63,

67,74,81,82,84,85,86,88,89,92,94,100,

1824 3,9,20,22,24,26,28,29,30,32,33,34,

35,36,38,39,40,41,42,48,52,54,57,58,65,66.

67,72,73,75,78,81,84,88,89,92,93,100,104,

1825 5,6,7,9,14,16,20,24,29,32,33,35,38,39

42,44,47,53,54,56,57,59,61,65,66,70,73,

77,84,85,86,88,90,91,92,94,97,98,99,101,

104,105,

1826 1,4,7,9,14,15,16,17,19,20,21,28,29,

32, 33,34,35,36,38,40,41,42,44,45,46,47,51,

60,61,65,66,73,75,81,84,85,86,91,94,101,103,

104,106,

1827 1,3,16,27,29,33,36,38,39,44,48,57,

61,62,81,84,86,87,94,104,105,

1828 1,15,16,17,22,24,39,43,44,50,55,64,

66,69,70,79,82,88,93,95,103,104,

1829 1.5,7,9,10,13,14,16,17,18,20,22,23,

29,30,35,36,39,42,43,44,45,46,48,52,54,56,

57,62,66,70,72,73,77,78,79,81,85,86,87,88,

92,95,97,99,102,104,105,